# SPIRITUAL TEACHINGS OF THE CHURCH

## *The History of Spirituality*

*By*

ELIZABETH RHYND

DIMENSION BOOKS
WILKES-BARRE, PENNSYLVANIA

*First Published* 1965.

© *Copyright by Clonmore and Reynolds Limited*

MADE AND PRINTED IN THE REPUBLIC OF IRELAND BY
HELY THOM LIMITED, DUBLIN, FOR CLONMORE AND REYNOLDS,
LIMITED. NIHIL OBSTAT: IOANNES ENGLISH, C.C., CENSOR
THEOL. DEPUT. IMPRIMI POTEST: ✠IOANNES CAROLUS,
ARCHIEP. DUBLINEN., HIBERNIAE PRIMAS. DUBLINI, DIE 30
NOVEMBER, 1964.

# CONTENTS

## PART ONE

## SHORT STUDIES IN MYSTICAL DIVERSITY

## PART TWO

## MEDIAEVAL PANORAMA

# ACKNOWLEDGEMENTS

AUTHOR AND publisher particularly wish to thank Burns &
Oates, London, and the Newman Press, Maryland, for their
kindness and co-operation in permitting such extensive use of
the material contained in the four volumes of Pourrat's *Christian
Spirituality*, also for their permission to quote from other translations owned by them. Details not included in the chapter notes
are given in the list of Sources.

Sincere thanks are also due to the following publishers in
Ireland, England and America for permission to use translations
of which they hold the copyright: Benziger Bros., New York;
B. Herder Book Company, St. Louis; Darton, Longman &
Todd, London; Sheed & Ward, London; Third Order Press,
Downers Grove, Illinois, P. J. Kenedy & Sons, New York; St.
Paul Publications, Langley, Bucks; The C.T.S., London;
Desclee Company, New York; The Harvill Press, London;
M. H. Gill & Son Ltd., Dublin. Full details of these publications,
in the order of reference, are given in the list of Sources and in
the chapter notes. Permission to quote from the Benedictine
translation of St. Teresa's *Interior Castle* was kindly given by
the Lady Abbess of Stanbrook Abbey.

# SOURCES OF QUOTATION

PIERRE POURRAT, S.S: *Christian Spirituality*, Vol. 1 (trans. W. H. Mitchell and S. P. Jacques), Vol. 2 (trans. S. P. Jacques), Vol. 3 (trans. W. H. Mitchell), Newman Press, Westminster, Maryland, 1953; Vol. 4 (trans. Donald Attwater), Newman Press, Westminster, Maryland, 1955.

MGR. ALBERT FARGES: *Mystical Phenomena* (trans. S.P. Jacques), Benziger, New York; Burns & Oates, London, 1926.

MATTHIAS SCHEEBEN: *Nature and Grace*, (trans. Cyril Vollert, S.J.), B. Herder Book Co., St. Louis, Mo., 1954. *Mysteries of Christianity*, (trans. Cyril Vollert, S.J.), B. Herder Book Co., St. Louis, Mo., 1946.

ST. JOHN OF THE CROSS: *Collected Works*, Vols. I & II (trans. D. Lewis), Longman, Green, Longman, Roberts & Green, 1864.

ST. TERESA OF AVILA: *Way of Perfection*, (trans. Benedictines of Stanbrook), Thomas Baker, London, 1925. *Interior Castle*, (trans. Benedictines of Stanbrook), Thomas Baker, London, 1921.

G. B. MONTINI: *Man's Religious Sense*, trans. and published Darton, Longman & Todd, London, 1957.

LUDOVICUS BLOSIUS: *Book of Spiritual Instruction*, (trans. from Latin by B. A. Wilberforce, O.P.), Newman Press, Maryland; Burns & Oates, London (Orchard Books Revised Edition, 1955).

JULIUS TYCIAK: *Life in Christ*, (trans. Basil Wrighton), Sheed & Ward, London, 1937.

ST. THOMAS AQUINAS: *Summa Theologica*, (trans. by the Fathers of the English Dominican Province, American Edition), Benziger Bros., Inc., New York, 1947.

THOR-SALVIAT, A. A: *Secrets of a Seraph*, (trans. G. N. Pausback, O.CARM.), Third Order Press, Downers Grove, Ill., 1961.

ANSCAR VONIER, O.S.B.: *Collected Works*, Vol. 2, Newman Press, Maryland; Burns & Oates, London, 1952. *Sketches & Studies in Theology*, Burns & Oates, London, 1940.

BARRY ULANOV (Ed.): *The Way of St. Alphonsus Liguori*, P. J. Kenedy & Sons, New York; Burns & Oates (Golden Library), London, 1960.

MGR. E. GUERRY: *In The Whole Christ*, English Edition, St. Paul Publications, Langley, Bucks, 1959.

C.T.S., London: *Papal Encyclicals* as given in chapter notes.

ANTONIO PIOLANTI: *The Holy Eucharist*, English Edition, Desclee Company, N.Y., 1961.

MGR. R. A. KNOX (Trans.): *Autobiography of a Saint*, Harvill Press, London, 1958.

GASTON COURTOIS: *The States of Perfection*, (trans. J. A. O'Flynn), M. H. Gill & Son Ltd., Dublin, 1961.

8

# INTRODUCTION

THIS BOOK appears to me to fulfil a definite need. Up to now, if one wanted to study spiritual theology in its development, one had either to search in many books or else to read Pourrat's *Christian Spirituality*. Either way, one was discouraged by the magnitude of the task. Pourrat is good, but his treatment of the subject is so diffuse that one cannot see the wood for the trees. It is of course most necessary that we read the mystical authors themselves, but I think it fair to say that there is still a widespread ignorance and even fear of such writings. One meets few, even among priests, who are at all versed in this field, and the outlook of most women religious is limited to their own experience.

Miss Rhynd's book, then, introduces us to a most fruitful field of study, and even if we lack the time to read all the originals mentioned, we shall learn a great deal from the synthesis itself. The author has read widely and in several languages. She is in touch with the best that has been written on her subject and distils her findings with a disarming simplicity. The sections devoted to St. Teresa and St. John of the Cross are especially noteworthy. Directors, as indeed all who are interested in the spiritual teaching of the Church, will find no more helpful guide to their reading than this present volume.

FR. NIVARD KINSELLA, O.C.S.O.

*Mount St. Joseph Abbey,*
*Roscrea,*
*Co. Tipperary.*

# THE GENERAL PLAN OF THE BOOK

MGR. ALBERT FARGES, in the introduction to his book *Mystical Phenomena*, makes the following statements:—

Mystical theology is a true science. Like all science worthy of the name, it is not only an accumulation of facts, but also a gathering together of explanatory theories founded on assured principles which are methodically bound into a single whole by means of reason. In fact every scientific system, like a living organism, is made up of three divisions: *unity* of the whole, *differentiation* of the parts, *synthesis* of the parts into the whole. Mystical theology is furthermore an experimental science. Nothing therein can be accused of being an "a priori" judgement: neither the facts which surpass human anticipation, nor the principles which are obtained from Christian revelation and by generalizing from the facts observed. . . .To seek to treat this science "a priori", then, would be to disfigure and even mutilate it.[1]

Unless these principles be kept in mind, it is impossible to pass beyond the limit of one's subjective preferences whilst studying the spirituality of the Catholic Church.

*Unity of the whole:* To find this, we must look to our Lord and Saviour Jesus Christ, the Word of God who united our human nature hypostatically to his own divine nature and person. "I am alpha and omega, the beginning and the end, saith the Lord God, who is and who was, and who is to come, the Almighty" (Apoc.i.8). While it is true that man can attain to a state of relative friendship with God the Father by means of natural knowledge, faith and love, and that this leads to conformity with the natural order that is in the world, it is still impossible for him to attain to justifying grace except first the Son of God stoop down to embrace the infirmity of his spirit, mind and flesh. As St. Cyril of Alexandria has said: "The bond of our union with God the Father is manifestly Christ, who has joined us to himself as man, but also to God, seeing that as God he is naturally in his Father. For a nature that is subject to corruption *could not be raised to incorruption* unless a nature that is free from all corruption and mutability had come down to it, elevating to its own condition of perfection the nature which ever remains inferior, extricating the latter so to speak from the limitations proper to the creature by joining and associating it with itself, and changing to conformity with itself the nature which inherently is not such."[2] Thus whatever experience a man may have of God, outside of Jesus Christ or of faith in the promise of his coming, is purely natural or philosophical in character; and that is why Mgr. Farges declares: "The first union of man with God, the highest, the most illuminating and most wonderful of all, is that of our Lord Jesus Christ himself, the God-man. It has shone over the whole earth, so that it has transformed the old world into a new one, and it will remain until the end of time the ideal proposed to all mystic saints for very far-off and imperfect imitation."[3]

*Differentiation of the parts:* The God-man did not wish to keep the divine life for himself alone. Had that been the case, it is unlikely that the Incarnation would ever have occurred. Infinite goodness is diffusive of its very nature, and for that reason we creatures are actually needed by God for the completion of his external glory. Our Lord therefore assures us that he has come to give us abundant life, and he desires that the fruits of this life shall be as a light shining before all men for the greater glory of his Father. Without the fore-knowledge that this could be achieved, he would not have founded a visible Church, "a city seated on a mountain" (Matt. v.14). As it is, however, the Church he founded is recognizable by her eminent holiness, not only in regard to doctrine and sacraments, but also by the heroic witness of thousands of her children. No two souls being identical, the manifestation of this inner union with Jesus Christ in so many different forms should not surprise us. Indeed, this diversity in unity is one of the greatest glories of the mystical body of our Redeemer.

*Synthesis of the parts:* This without doubt is the most delicate task for the spiritual theologian, and it is here that the danger of disfigurement or even of mutilation is at its greatest. The Church has given us relatively little authoritative teaching about mystical experience to guide our thinking—apart from assuring us of her predilection for the teaching of St. Teresa of Jesus and St. John of the Cross—so the success of any individual effort in this direction must necessarily be subject to the will of the Holy Spirit in manifesting the synthetic picture eternally present to the mind of Jesus Crucified. Humility, patience, restraint, gratitude above all for the painstaking efforts of theologians and historians in the past, these should be the marks of any truly scientific research into the glories of Christian spirituality.

*Method to be adopted:* The object of this present short work is threefold: firstly, to draw attention to the essential features of the various kinds of mystical experience manifested during the first fifteen centuries of the Christian era; secondly, to demonstrate the extent to which St. Teresa of Jesus and St. John of the Cross were the living embodiment of all these experiences; thirdly, to show how spiritual doctrine has been affected by the trials afflicting the Church between the sixteenth century and this present time. From this objective study we may be able to draw a few tentative conclusions—especially as the mystery of the hypostatic union in our Lord remains at the heart of prayer and contemplative experience in every age—but we shall not presume to complete the synthesis, since the end of the story must necessarily await the eternal nuptials in heaven of the Lamb with his Bride. Through the merits of his Passion may he grant us all the grace to participate in this climax of his Incarnation, a reward promised to those who prove their love for him by keeping his commandments here below, Amen.

[1]A. Farges, *Mystical Phenomena*, p. 1.

[2]In Joann. lib. XI, c.12. See also Matthias Scheeben on the "Spiritual Nature of Man" and on "Faith" in *Nature and Grace*, pp. 70–98 and 235–44. Further important passages pertaining to this subject occur in Scheeben's *Mysteries of Christianity*, pp. 396–7, 416–7, 541 and 632–3, to mention but a few of the most striking examples.

[3]A. Farges, *Mystical Phenomena*, p. 19.

## PART ONE

# SHORT STUDIES IN MYSTICAL DIVERSITY

## 1   THE SPIRIT OF THE APOSTLES

OUR LORD promised at the Last Supper that even greater marvels than those effected during his life on earth would be manifested through the members of his mystical body after he had ascended to his Father. Because it is the mission of the Holy Ghost to glorify the Son through the witness of the Church, so is this made possible. Without the divine assistance, on the other hand, the Church could not have survived the persecutions of the first three centuries. Indeed the miraculous element during this period is particularly noticeable, this being necessary for the instruction of the heathen in the sense that they were "aliens from the conversation of Israel, and strangers to the testament, having no hope in the promise, and without God in this world" (Ephes. ii.12). Thus St. Paul in his first epistle to the Corinthians refers at length to the different manifestations of the Spirit (xii. 7-11), but he is careful to insist in the following chapter that the power to effect marvels has no Christian meaning apart from charity, apart that is from the life of sanctifying grace which comes to us in Christ Jesus our Lord. This man Paul, who had himself been rapt to the third heaven in a miraculous vision of the divine essence (a vision lower in degree only from the full beatific vision), had no illusions on this point; and so we find that the whole of his teaching to the Gentiles is concerned with the demonstration of what it means *in practice* to be regenerated through baptism in Christ. Sacramental grace apart, St. Paul's concept of identification with the Master involves the mortification of the Cross and the imitation of his virtues, then active union with him in faith, in hope and in love; and this important distinction between sacramental and actual grace is emphasized by Père Pourrat when he writes: "Christian life is the result of a twofold operation: that of God who makes us conformable to the image of his Son; and our own whereby we produce that image within us. . . . If the Christian is incorporated into the Saviour by divine grace, it is his duty to make his life conform with Christ's and to imitate him. The members who make up the mystical body of Christ would be unfaithful to their calling, if they did not reproduce the likeness of their Head as perfectly as possible within themselves."[1]

In the case of St. John, the seer of Patmos, who by the grace of infused knowledge was granted the comprehension of heavenly secrets unknown to the minds of ordinary Christians, it was the will of God to use him as *the instrument* of manifestation in regard to these high matters; but even so he might have fallen from essential grace, had he not made it his first concern to keep the commandments of the Master, in particular the commandment of love as given at the Last Supper. All the writings of St. John in his gospel and epistles are devoted to the elucidation of these basic doctrines of faith and love and the supernatural vigour which comes to us through our incorporation with Jesus the true Vine, firstly by baptism and the holy Eucharist, secondly by constant prayer and dependence on the Master, by the performance of meritorious acts, and by patience in the hour of suffering.

By temperament, no two saints could have been more different: John the son of Zebedee the fisherman, Paul the brilliant intellectual trained by Gamaliel in the school of the Pharisees: and the nature of each had to be elevated by the Holy Spirit according to its own particular characteristics, strength, weakness and interior inclination. With varying degrees of complexity, this same principle applies to the interior fashioning of all the apostles, as indeed of every saint and spiritual writer whose name will be cited in the course of this brief survey; so— once again—let us not be surprised by so great a diversity. If we desire to find a principle of unity, apart from Jesus himself and the mediation of his Virgin Mother, then it is to *the fundamental practice of infused virtue* in these men and women that we must look, above all to their heroic spirit of faith, hope and charity. A prudent Christian will never desire to experience extraordinary phenomena, yet he cannot prevent these manifestations if God so wills them. In so far as they do occur, the important point to realize is that they are given for the edification of the weak, the ignorant and the unbelieving, rather than for the benefit of the visionary thus favoured. If we remember this, we shall not go far astray in examining the evidence of our senses.


2   THE MARTYRS OF THE FIRST THREE CENTURIES

Whilst the pagan persecutions lasted, the general level of supernatural virtue in the Christian communities remained extraordinarily high, not least in regard to consecrated virginity which was the glory both of the women and of so many men as well. The explanation of this is easy to discern, for as Pourrat writes: "Jesus was to the first Christians no abstract ideal. The very definite feeling of his presence in the Church and in the hearts of the faithful was everywhere displayed. The outward and striking return of Christ not being realized, as so many expected, more especial attention was given to his spiritual and mysterious presence in the soul."[2] The writings of St. Ignatius of Antioch and St. Irenaeus are steeped in this thought of the closeness of the union between Christ and his members, a union which gives them "the strength to persevere in humility and in complete purity and perfect temperance of body and soul".[3] Those undergoing martyrdom were frequently strengthened by ecstasy and by other foretastes of the perfect union awaiting them in heaven. In the hour of their torment, it was clear to all that "the Saviour was by their side and held communion with them",[4] also that their one fear was to be deprived of so glorious a death. "Let no creature, visible or invisible, try in jealousy to snatch me from Christ Jesus!" exclaimed St. Ignatius of Antioch, "Come fire and cross, fighting tooth and claw with wild beasts, let me be cut to pieces alive, dismembered and disjointed, and my whole body ground to powder, and the cruellest tortures of the devil inflicted upon me, provided that I gain Christ in the end!" St. Stephen, the deacon, had been the first of the martyrs to enter heaven (Acts vii. 54-9), then countless others such as St. Perpetua and her brother St. Saturus, St. Cyprian, St. Pionius, St. Marianus, St. James, St. Lawrence, St. Polycarp, St. Flavian, St. Blandina. The manifest gifts of prophecy and of impassibility were even more remarkable than the various visions and ecstasies experienced, also the fact that the wild beasts sometimes became tame and the torturing flames powerless to burn. Truly there is no power in heaven or on earth which the humanity of Jesus Christ cannot restrain if his Father so wills.

## 3   THE ABSTRACT APPROACH OF THE MYSTICAL PHILOSOPHERS

It has always been the practice of the Church to Christianize the pagan philosophies and to emphasize the points of agreement as far as possible. This process is not without its dangers for the Christian thinker, especially as it leads him so far into the field of the abstract and may alienate him from that simple awareness of Jesus Christ which dominated the lives of the apostles and martyrs, but it is no less essential for the safeguarding of the Church against intellectual error. Further, it has proved possible for men of genius—like St. Augustine, St. Dionysius the Areopagite, and later St. Thomas Aquinas—not only to succeed on rational lines, but even to give to the Church some of her deepest concepts of supernatural mysticism. It is of value therefore to note the different ways in which the Church's ideals have been attacked, the manner in which they have been defended, and also the higher truths which have emerged from these intellectual conflicts. No progress has ever been made in the spread of the Christian religion without either persecution from the enemies of the Church or the threat of heretical teaching from within.

Best known amongst the different forms of heterodox asceticism affecting the early Church were *Gnosticism* and *Neoplatonism*, the latter having originated in the pre-Christian philosophy of the Greeks, spreading thence to the famous centre of learning in Alexandria. A preliminary word, however, should be added about *Encratism* and *Montanism* as found during the previous century.

The Encratites strove primarily to destroy the normal balance of Christian mortification and asceticism by seeking to impose celibacy on every man and woman, together with perpetual abstinence from meat and wine, on the grounds that these measures were necessary for salvation. The need to react strongly against pagan immorality, together with the natural pride and delight which some people take in the works of austerity, enabled this fanatical spirit to gain considerable foothold, and it was not until the beginning of the third century that the system was finally declared heretical. Meantime the illuministic doctrine of Montanus had been developed in

2

Phrygia, Africa and Lyons, adding to the ascetical exaggerations of the Encratites an ecstatic form of mysticism said to be associated with the dominion of the Paraclete in preparation for the end of the world. This variety of private enlightenment, however, was pitted against ecclesiastical authority, and before long it too was declared heretical.

The Hellenic philosophy, in which gnosticism originated, comprised initially the dualism of Philo and the preceding philosophers of the Graeco-Roman world, but gradually it came to include a mixture of Judaism and Christianity as well. The gnostic philosophy looked upon the flesh as diametrically opposed to the welfare of the spirit, and adapted its ascetical programme accordingly. Neoplatonism, on the other hand, although it frequently utilized gnostic methods of gaining self-mastery, was concerned more particularly with the attainment of divine union in the natural, pantheistic sense of the term. Ecstatic contemplation was regarded as the supreme means of identifying the soul with God himself, consequently of receiving habitual illumination from above; hence its great attraction for men of strong intellect.

Clement of Alexandria (A.D. 150-217) admired the Greek philosophies so much that he tried to give a new meaning to the term "gnosis", interpreting this as a "consummation of faith", a privilege whereby souls are granted "superessential intuitions" in regard to the divine truths which ordinary Christians accept blindly. Further, he claimed that this consummation could be achieved in a twofold way: first, through concentrating on "the negative idea of God" (as later developed by St. Augustine and St. Dionysius the Areopagite) since reason cannot serve as a proximate means of union with him; secondly, through a combination of stoical insensibility and Christian charity for the purpose of acquiring a closer resemblance to God. Clement however, for all his stoicism, did not urge the practice of virginity. He recognized the superiority of the virginal state over that of marriage, but he seemed to be of the opinion that few were capable of it.

Origen, the famous disciple of Clement (d. 254), also measured the quality of a man's life by the degree of his knowledge, but he realized that perfection or likeness to God depends basically on the moral order, therefore that personal effort—if not assisted by God—will not suffice. He urged the practice of perfect chastity and virginity almost to the point of depreciating the married state, and even went so far as to mutilate his own body at the age of eighteen. With unrelenting will-power he drove himself to maintain a life of prayer and fasting and the strictest evangelical poverty possible. The men he trained were taught to regard themselves as strict contemplatives rather than as workers, whilst he himself longed only to dwell in the wilderness "where the air was purer, the sky more open, and God nearer".[6] Certainly the influence he exerted was very great and is said to have accounted for the amazing spread of monachism in heathen Egypt.

The neoplatonic use of the term "union with God" is so misleading that it is well to stress again its non-Christian character. Natural virtue can go a very long way towards harmonizing the mind and heart of man with his Creator, and unless we appreciate this point we shall always feel bewildered by the claims of ascetics and contemplatives outside the Church. We have to be on our guard, too, against the modern tendency to deny the existence of the natural order. This point of view is based on the idea that since all men are called to participate in the same supernatural destiny, they must therefore be subject to the same supernatural influences; but we have only to read the epistles of St. Paul in the light of Christ's own words to the Jews, in order to see that the Church has been at pains from the very beginning to "distinguish between two orders of knowledge and truth, as

well as between two kinds of ethically good actions in man".[7]
These last words from Scheeben's *Nature and Grace* provide the
key to many complexities in the intellectual order.

During the first two years after his baptism in 388, St.
Augustine discovered that the neoplatonic theory of contemplation corresponded closely with his own experience at the time,
and so he made extensive use of its philosophical terminology
in his own writings. As his soul matured, he came to value the
light of faith increasingly, also the role of theological hope and
charity. At first, however, it seemed to him that moral preparation
was paramount, together with the ardent desires of the mind for
divine illumination or the vision of truth.

Concerning this vision of truth, Pourrat assembles the following key points from the writings of St. Augustine:—

> The contemplation of Supreme Goodness discloses the vanity of
> earthly things, and explains the disillusionment of the sacred
> writer proclaiming the nothingness of everything under the
> sun.[8]

> The first mark of contemplation is the suspension of the faculties
> of the soul, which become bound. Everything consists in the
> simple seeing of the soul which is plunged in celestial light . . .
> a kind of ecstasy by which the intellectual vision of God is
> procured, and by which God communes directly with the soul.[9]

> The truths of faith are shown to the soul in so bright a daylight
> and become so evident that it seems to have known nothing
> before, so small was the knowledge of them compared to that
> which comes to it with contemplation.[10]

Here we have evidence not only of abundant infused light
but also of the gifts of knowledge, wisdom and understanding,
according to their ordinary mode of co-operation with faith in
the active intelligence—a perfect example of the doctrine of
the monk Hesychius as contained in the following passage: "At

the beginning of its sanctification, the light given to the soul may be compared with that of a lamp which guides it in the way of goodness and leads it safely through dangers. Then the light grows greater and brighter. The soul is as completely environed with it as if it were that of the moon at full. Lastly, Jesus himself like a radiant sun appears to the soul in his wonderful perfections, inundating it with his heavenly light. Then comes an ineffable contemplation of divine truths."[11]

Of St. Augustine as a theologian and doctor of the Church we shall treat later. For the present, let us simply note that "mystical contemplation" in the Augustinian sense of the term has a twofold signification: firstly, the illumination of the intellect by means of faith and the gifts; secondly, the connatural enjoyment of the will and subsequent tendency towards affective ecstasy. The aspirations of the neoplatonists were not dissimilar, but in their case the supernatural means of arriving at the desired goal had not yet been granted to them; therefore they had to fall back on their own moral and intellectual efforts in the attempt to make progress.

Complementary to the mystical teaching of St. Augustine is the more obscure doctrine of St. Dionysius the Areopagite— more obscure because it treats of the conduct of the Christian soul if raised by God to the passive states of prayer. In this context, the knowledge of God attainable through reason is called "demonstrative" or "philosophical" theology; that which comes by supernatural intuition is called "mystical" theology. The intermediate stage, wherein faith and reason operate to- gether (as is the case with the majority of Christian souls in every age), does not form part of the Dionysian doctrine as such. For that, we must refer back to St. Augustine and all the other great exponents of Catholic dogma. St. Dionysius, then, teaches that mystical theology is superior to demonstrative theology, being a free gift and fruit of divine inspiration calculated to enlighten and instruct the soul in such a way that it no longer relies on reason or seeks truth by laborious methods. By way of remote preparation for this divine favour (should our Lord see fit to grant it), the soul must exercise itself constantly in mortification and virtue, at the same time pursuing a life of prayer. We must note, however, that the desired theopathic state may not be granted, and that any attempt to induce this state has the immediate effect of exposing the soul to the dangers of illuminism or quietistic apathy. Always the doctrine of the mystics has to be interpreted against the background of the Church's teaching as a whole, and the urge to generalize from advice given to one particular soul or group of souls must be avoided at all costs. St. Dionysius himself was aware that his teaching could not be practised indiscriminately, and St. John of the Cross was later to establish the "three signs" whereby the soul might know if it had been placed by God in the path of obscure contemplation;[12] yet innumerable are the would-be mystics who have regarded *the desire* for the infused touches of union as an infallible sign that they have but to shut their eyes, abandon all interior effort, and simply wait for them to occur. St. Teresa was to warn her daughters repeatedly against the dangers of exaggerated absorption and pseudo-ecstasy which merely weaken the body and endanger the balance of the mind, declaring all this to be great spiritual foolishness.[13] Indeed, not even through prayer have we any claim on the mystical contemplation described by St. Dionysius, neither can it be regarded as a reward for virtue (as is sometimes the case with Augustinian contemplation); only God knows why it is suited to the sanctification of some souls, yet apparently not to the majority.

Another practical difficulty about the Dionysian teaching is that so few writers of this school distinguish between "the work of God" and "the work of the soul" in the matter of detachment from temporal and spiritual goods. In practice, the greater part of this detachment is effected passively in the soul; and if this were not the case, the soul would not yet be ripe to depart from the ordinary ways of the spiritual life. It must however *consent* to this process of interior despoiling, and it must be careful *not to replace* earthly pleasures by clinging to sensible consolations, visions, locutions and the like. Thus the process of nescience, established in the first place by the direct action of pure faith in the intellect, has *yet to be completed* by the deliberate rejection of every spiritual or preternatural experience that is less than God himself. Such is the programme subsequently laid down by St. John of the Cross in the *Ascent of Mount Carmel*,[14] and this too is the meaning of the more obscure teaching of St. Dionysius to his disciple Timothy. If we imagine that it is the soul who should take the initiative in bringing itself to nothing in this interior way, we shall be lucky if we retain our sanity at all, let alone our physical health.

The teaching of St. Augustine is not concerned with these particular difficulties, because the soul in his contemplative picture—whatever its happy experience of infused light—still retains the vital control of its faculties, ascending rather than descending to the revelation of God as he really is, and the contemplation granted does not involve the infused impressed species peculiar to the Dionysian experience.[15] In other words, the light given gratuitously to St. Augustine enabled him to contemplate wordlessly the knowledge of God already stored in his memory; whereas, in the case of St. Dionysius, this infused light was associated with the intuition of those substantial acts of God whereby he reveals his essential presence in the depths of the soul. This is what is meant by the term "sensation of the divine" or *patiens divina*, the effect in the soul of the *infused impressed species* of contemplation according to the extraordinary mode of the gifts of wisdom and understanding.[16] Entrance into the divine obscurity through union of the will, together with a

progressive ligature of the understanding and memory during
times of prayer, these are the stages which precede the substantial
manifestation of God to the soul. This experience, however, is
not to be identified with the beatific vision, not even in the degree
granted to Moses and St. Paul; it is as yet no more than the
intuition of the angels, also it requires the mediation of the
Word Incarnate. The human personality, moreover, is never
"lost" or "merged" in the divinity of God as desired by the
neoplatonists.

To many people, this teaching about infused impressed
species seems totally incomprehensible. Nonetheless it occurs
again in the writings of St. Thomas Aquinas, the greatest of all
abstract thinkers,[17] and can be understood, analogously at least,
by studying the scholastic theory of knowledge. In Dionysian
contemplation, faith is still the medium of the infused light,
whereas faith in the life to come will be replaced by the created
light of glory.

## 4  THE CONTEMPLATIVES OF THE DESERT

The dying down of pagan persecution by the end of the third
century led directly to moral slackness in the Christian communities, and for this reason it became imperative to safeguard
the welfare of virgins and ascetics. Already some legislation had
been introduced by the bishops, but that did not suffice, and so
began the steady exodus into the solitudes of the desert. Pourrat
supplies a vivid description of contemplative life as it gradually
took shape in Egypt and Palestine, then in northern Syria and
Mesopotamia, finally in Asia Minor,[18] and he also gives an
interesting account of the Rule of St. Pachomius followed by that
of St. Basil[19] which remains to this day in all the Greco-Slavonic
religious houses. In Egypt and Palestine, Syria and Mesopotamia,

asceticism was carried to unprecedented extremes, and in some cases the gifts of healing and prophecy were also manifested. In these countries, hermits were very numerous, but in Asia Minor under St. Basil the coenobitic Rule of St. Pachomius was developed and adapted until gradually it supplanted all other forms of religious profession. By the fifth century, four classes of monks were known to the Christian world: the coenobites, the hermits, the sarabaites (who had no rule but lived together in small groups), and the *gyrovagi* or vagabonds.

Religious instruction prior to the fourth century was handed down, for the most part, orally and by example. After that, however, some genuine treatises on monastic asceticism began to appear. The most outstanding of the writers of this period were: St. Nilus of Mount Sinai, St. Ephraem of Edessa, and St. John Chrysostom: men who regarded the interior of the soul largely as a battleground. Many of those who embraced the coenobitic ideal had been criminals or robbers prior to their conversion, a fact which must be taken into account when considering the ruthless forms of mortification and penance then in vogue. The precise character of religious life has always to adapt itself to the social conditions prevailing at any given time, and the element of fear in these early monasteries was not so overwhelming that the virtues of faith, hope and charity could not be developed simultaneously. It was taught, for example, that "to partake of food and even of wine to a reasonable extent is better than fasting and drinking water with pride";[20] and St. Anthony used to urge his monks on the following lines: "He who would be truly virtuous and who desires to attain the heights of perfection, will watch his brethren and endeavour to imitate the virtue in which each excels. One is remarkable for his gentleness, another for his love of prayer, a third for his chastity. Like the bee, the monk will pilfer to some extent in all directions to make spiritual honey for the improvement and sustenance of his soul."[21] Again, he used to say: "A clean life and lively faith are weapons dreaded by the demons. . . . Satan fears, in those who lead good lives, vigils, prayers, fasts, gentleness, voluntary poverty, contempt for vainglory, humility, mercy, control of one's temper and above all a heart filled with the love of Christ."[22]

On the subject of monastic prayer, St. Nilus, Cassian and Hesychius were the principal writers during the fourth and fifth centuries, and it is noteworthy to what extent they insisted that a dry feather will "easily fly upwards" whereas one with "a little water on it . . . becomes heavy and remains on the ground".[23] This practical connexion between progress in prayer and the consistent practice of virtue became a theme especially dear to St. Teresa and to all the great Carmelites. Those who maintained that work was contrary to the spirit of contemplation were denounced by St. Nilus from the summit of Mount Sinai on the grounds that such an attitude was contrary to the spirit of fraternal charity, and this too is a point of great importance for the proper understanding of mystical prayer. Both St. John Chrysostom and St. Jerome regarded the priesthood as even more exalted than the monastic calling—in marked contrast with St. Pachomius who regarded the priesthood, for monks, as a source of temptation to pride and ambition—and they further insisted on the virtues of learning and eloquence if the priests were to do justice to the sacred functions entrusted to them. To this end, manual labour and penance alone do not suffice.

Of the various monastic centres detailed by Pourrat, the one founded on Mount Sinai by St. Nilus became the most famous, due it seems to the outstanding government of St. John Climacus, author of *The Ladder of Paradise* and the *Book of the Pastor*. Numerous hermits lived in the neighbourhood as well, but this type of life was only permitted to those who were spiritually advanced. The practice of private confession was strongly advocated by St. John Climacus, and also at this time there was a notable increase in monastic devotion to the Mother of God.

The teaching contained in *The Ladder of Paradise* resembles the interior doctrine of St. Augustine in many ways. Further, by summarizing the spirituality of his forerunners, St. John Climacus (525–600) gave to Greek ascetic theology the same kind of practical synthesis as did St. John Damascene in the case of dogmatic theology. The thirty steps of the Ladder correspond with the thirty years of our Lord's hidden life in Nazareth, each being covered by a separate chapter of the book. Steps 1–7 deal with the virtues and vices pertaining to beginners and are primarily concerned with the obtaining of monastic fervour through detachment from earthly things. Steps 8–27 show how the interior combat intensifies, culminating however in freedom from all evil inclinations and in mastery of the passions. Steps 28–30 describe the solitude, apatheia and divine union of the perfect. In general, one can remark that St. John Climacus laid special stress on the sanctifying power of perfect obedience, also on the importance of humble confession and of fatherly dispositions in those who hear the confessions of the brethren. His ideas about reparation, on the other hand, seem unduly severe by modern standards. There were no half-measures about these Eastern monks, and interior progress is always considered in terms of victory over the devil and man's lower nature.[24] The anchorite or hermit is regarded as superior to the coenobite, but is expected to live as though his body had ceased to exist, thus enabling his soul to be enkindled, enlightened, and finally purified by divine fire. While it is true that St. John Climacus made this exalted state of apatheia depend on the practice of every virtue, his teaching on this subject has often been criticized by reason of its stoical flavour. Psychologically, such a state of mind is often found in those who practise the affective contemplation described by St. John of the Cross in the first chapter of the *Obscure*

*Night, I,* but it does not bear any resemblance to the apatheia of the Teresian transforming union. Curiously, too, St. John Climacus does not treat of the theological virtues prior to his thirtieth step. He does not deny that these virtues "unite most closely all the parts of the mystical ladder",[25] but he seems to regard them as an end in themselves rather than the means whereby we draw close to the indwelling presence of God. Again, the climax of the mystical life for St. John Climacus seems to resemble the miraculous form of essential vision as experienced by Moses and St. Paul, and the following description is fully characteristic of the spirituality of the East: "When the soul is immersed in, and entirely penetrated by charity, a kind of splendour radiates from it, like the glory which shone round Moses when he descended from Mount Sinai. In this angelic degree of charity, man forgets to take food and hardly feels the need for it. He is nourished invisibly by the fire of love, like roots of plants fed by water beneath the ground."[26] Such achievements in spiritualization are truly remarkable, but they are not in any way essential to interior perfection. In his *Book of the Pastor,* on the other hand, St. John Climacus gives such beautiful teaching concerning the qualities which a superior of a monastery should possess, that many regard this as more valuable than the mystical doctrine which he intended for anchorites.

In contrast with the spirituality of Mount Sinai is the Christological doctrine of that great martyr of the Monothelite heresy, St. Maximus the Confessor (580–662), at one time secretary to Emperor Heraclius. About the year 630, he left the imperial court because of the favour shown by Heraclius to the Monothelite heresy, and became abbot of the convent of Chrysopolis on the far side of the Bosphorus. Then some fifteen years later, Pourrat tells us, "he nonplussed Pyrrhus, the Monothelite ex-patriarch of Constantinople" at a solemn conference held at Carthage in north Africa. Thence "returning to Rome, he persuaded Pope St. Martin I to call the celebrated Council of the Lateran together, which anathematized Monothelitism and its adherents, amongst whom were the emperors Heraclius and Constantine II".[27] The pope was subsequently arrested and died in 635 while still in exile. St. Maximus on the other hand, along with two of his disciples, was "condemned to be scourged, to have the right hand cut off and the tongue pulled out" with the result that these heroes of the Faith "died from the sufferings they went through in A.D. 662".[28]

Known best as a valiant defender of Catholic dogma, St. Maximus was also a deeply spiritual man and a keen theologian, devoted to all the mysteries of the Incarnate Word. Further, he accepted the Dionysian theories concerning affirmative and negative theology; but the key to his own spirituality is to be found in his devotion to the Sacred Humanity, and it is this living synthesis of the *abstract* and the *personal* which makes his theology so outstanding. It is true that the end of contemplation is union with God, also that this deification is brought about by charity; but he taught that this assimilation of the human will to the divine is realized *initially* in Christ. The Monothelites rejected the doctrine of the two wills in the Incarnate Word—probably through failing to realize that Christ's human will was distinct *as a power* even although one with the Father *as the instrument* of the divine purposes—and in this way they made inexplicable the whole mystery of the deification of man fallen and redeemed. In modern times, the tendency is not so much to deny the teaching of the Church on this point, as to ignore its practical import for ourselves, and this applies especially to the theology of the Eucharist. As Pourrat truly says, referring to the teaching of St. Maximus: "The Incarnation is the great event of the world, which God ordained from the beginning and which makes the object of creation possible. It is why Christ unites everything in himself, in the same way as the Church unites within herself all the different nations of which she is composed."[29]

## 5   DEFENDERS OF THE FAITH

Since the glories of Christian dogma and spirituality are usually made prominent by those very heresies and exaggerations which seek to destroy them, it follows that the Church has need at all times of skilled theologians to defend the truth. Great as the asceticism of the Desert may be, it does not save the mind of man from intellectual error, and both the Monophysite and Mono-thelite heresies owed their widespread influence to ignorance rather than to ill-will. We must therefore go back a little and note the struggle between St. Augustine and Pelagius as to the power and moral worth of human nature when unaided by supernatural grace.

Pelagianism, in seeking to exalt man's nature and spiritual potentialities independently of grace, struck at the very heart of the hypostatic mystery in Jesus Christ our mystical Head, just as Luther, Baius and Jansenius did a thousand years later—at the opposite extreme—by insisting on the corruption of the natural soul in its substance, in its faculties, or in its inclinations. The Augustinian view, which the Church adopted from the beginning, distinguishes clearly between man's power to work for *a natural end* and his power to achieve *the supernatural destiny* intended for him. Even without grace, the former power remains in some measure; but the latter capacity is totally lost until grace is given or restored through the gratuitous mercy of God.[30]

Pelagius himself, a man of robust constitution and great austerity, was born in Britain and later became a monk. After travelling in the East, he settled in Rome about the year 400, and was considered to be a man of great virtue until St. Augustine began to see through his errors and to warn people accordingly. He was condemned as a heretic by Pope Zosimus in the year 418.

The seeds of the Pelagian heresy can be discerned initially in the stoicism of Zeno, then in the Alexandrian gnostic ideal of ascetical insensibility, finally in that form of monastic pride which claimed to be independent of the divine assistance and capable of doing all things involving moral effort through sheer will-power. According to Pelagius, the gift of free-will provides man with the power to do good on his own: "To be good, it is enough to will it and take trouble to be it. Our will is all-powerful for good. To appeal to the grace of God in aid of our assumed impotence is an act of cowardice."[31] His subsequent spirituality was full of rigorism and pride, as might be expected, and he had many followers including a monk named Celestius and Julian, Bishop of Eclanum in Apulia.

St. Augustine began his refutation of Pelagian doctrine about the year 414, assisted for a time by St. Jerome, and he continued with it until death overtook him sixteen years later. He was directly responsible for the condemnation of Celestius and Julian, above all through the part which he played in the great Council of Carthage. He also replied to the semi-pelagianism of the monks of Hadrumetum in Africa, Lerins and Marseilles, who thought that he was exaggerating man's helplessness and so giving rise to a spirit of fatalistic indifference. Further, these monks protested that if everything depended on God, then they themselves could not be held responsible if they became lazy and committed faults. To this, St. Augustine replied to the effect that "the power to pray, when made use of, acquires the power to act".[32]

The spiritual teaching of St. Augustine is summarized by Pourrat at considerable length.[33] Here, it suffices if we note the following points:—

*a)* The *basis* of Christian perfection is humility and faith, its *term* is perfect charity. The greater our love of God, the happier and more perfect we become; therefore progress in these virtues is the essential law of our interior life.

*b)* *Progress* is made in a threefold way: by conquest of the flesh, by our consistent practice of all the virtues, and by prayer. The emphasis of St. Augustine on the role of faith, hope and charity is very striking, above all in relation to Jesus Christ our Saviour, our model for every action required of us here below.

*c)* The *growth* of charity reveals four stages, and St. Augustine thinks of this development as being in the spirit of the Gradual Psalms which the Jews used to chant during their ascent to the holy city of Jerusalem. This charity, moreover, tends towards union; it "desires to be but one with the object loved".[34]

*d)* *Temptation*, in the mind of St. Augustine, signified enticement to evil rather than a positive means towards progress in virtue. It is, in fact, one of the principal means whereby our tendency to pride and pelagian self-sufficiency is undermined; but St. Augustine belonged to an age that believed in the repression or stamping out of evil within the human soul (almost as though it had some existence of its own), and for that reason his policy was one of immediate flight from the occasion of disturbance. Acts of calling upon Christ and remembering his teaching, of putting confidence in his grace and of yearning for heaven, these too he advocated, together with fasting and the continual practice of the presence of God. The main difference between this and the teaching of the Desert Fathers on temptation is that St. Augustine attributes very much less to the direct agency of the devil. Instead, he blames man's own fallen nature and concupiscence together with the influence of the world.

Most striking of all, however, is the example and teaching of St. Augustine on fraternal charity, for which reason he is known as the "Doctor of Charity" and is often represented holding a heart. St. Mary Magdalene of Pazzi, in the sixteenth century, was to model her life closely on Augustinian lines, similarly the Carmelite of Dijon, Sister Elizabeth of the Trinity, during the first years of the twentieth century. The supernatural reasoning of St. Thérèse of Lisieux on the subject of charity was probably more original.

Considering the vital importance of devotion to the Sacred Humanity during the first centuries of the Church's life, it comes as no surprise that Satan should make such frequent attacks on the doctrines upon which this devotion is based. Only thus could he hope to prevent, or at least to hinder, the further spread of Christ's kingdom on earth; and yet, in practice, his efforts served only to strengthen the position of the Church all the more. Each attempted heresy led to a further unfolding of the divine truth contained in the deposit of faith handed down from the apostles, subsequently to new degrees of Christological devotion. The intellectual genius of St. Augustine, up to the year of his death, embraced nearly every dogma, above all the mysteries of the Incarnation; then after him in the East came St. Cyril of Alexandria, following in the wake of St. Athanasius, defender of the Faith against the Arian heresy. St. Cyril at the Council of Ephesus was champion both of "the Personal Unity of Christ" and of "the Divine Maternity of our Lady"; then, in the West, came Pope St. Leo the Great with his magnificent dogmatic homilies. The distinction between the two natures in Christ was *defined* after the condemnation of Eutyches at the Council of Chalcedon in the year 451, and this resulted in a still more glorious flowering of the Church's love for Mary and her divine Son.

St. Augustine was the first doctor of the Church to develop in full the basic doctrine concerning the mystical body of Christ, and he repeatedly stressed the fact that the Word "in uniting himself *hypostatically* to human nature, is also united *spiritually* to each one of us".[35] This identity of Christ with his mystical

3

body means so much to St. Augustine that he reverts to it time and again in his homilies and other writings. With St. Athanasius and St. Cyril, on the other hand, the emphasis is more particularly on the necessity of the Incarnation, for our sanctification as well as for our basic salvation.

During the fourth and fifth centuries, as a direct outcome of the controversies with Arians and Nestorians, the mysteries of the Eucharist received a prominence hitherto unknown. If Christ were not God, or if his Sacred Humanity had ever existed independently of the Word, then his flesh which we receive in Holy Communion could not transmit the divine life to us. Again, if there had been "only a moral, accidental union between the person of the Word and our human nature, as Nestorius held",[36] the flesh of Christ would have been human rather than divine and of no benefit to ourselves. The hypostatic union between the flesh of Christ and the person of the Word is of such import to the life of the Church, that even to this day we find efforts being made to belittle its significance or to make the faithful believe that the earthly Humanity is unworthy of their love and contemplation. In reality, the eucharistic flesh of Jesus is the one food adapted to the weakness and frailty of man during his earthly pilgrimage, and it vivifies him like a divine fire. "As soon as he enters into us by Communion," Pourrat says quoting Hesychius, "he drives from our hearts the spirit of malice, effaces our sins, and preserves our souls from evil thoughts. If afterwards we are careful to guard our hearts and keep them shut against all evil, when we again approach the holy mysteries, the divine body will impregnate our souls with more and more light, making them to shine like stars."[37]

Devotion to the Mother of God during the first centuries of the Church's life was shown forth, as we have seen, by the practice of virginity and similar imitation of all the Marian virtues. St. Ambrose and St. Jerome in the West, St. Augustine and St.

Ephraem in the East never wearied of extolling the holiness of Mary. St. Irenaeus and Tertullian, too, looked upon her as their "deliverer"; and St. Cyril of Alexandria has attributed it to Mary that "Christian churches have been founded in towns, villages and islands . . . that every faithful soul is saved".[38] With the definition of the dogma of the Divine Maternity in 431, following the condemnation of Nestorius, devotion to Mary received the same stimulus as did devotion to the Sacred Humanity of her Son; and this was the signal for yet more remarkable developments in the spiritual life of the times.

## 6 THE FIRST MONASTIC FOUNDERS IN THE WESTERN CHURCH

Small communities of celibates, in Rome particularly, had existed in the West even before the fourth century. Later, about the year 335, St. Athanasius (the historian of St. Antony) was exiled from the East on account of his opposition to the Arian heresy, and stayed in Rome for some time on his way to Trèves. Thus was effected the first major link between the West and the religious life of the East, one to be followed by visits from Paulinus of Antioch and Epiphanius of Salamis. Pilgrims to Palestine, Egypt and Syria had the opportunity of observing monastic practices for themselves, and St. Augustine while still a pagan was also influenced in this way. St. Just of Lyons even left his episcopal see in order to end his days as a monk in Egypt. Both St. Jerome and St. Ambrose of Milan exerted unprecedented influence in the matter of persuading souls to adopt a life of consecrated virginity; but whereas St. Jerome's approach was essentially inspired by the example of the saints of the desert, St. Ambrose was more concerned with the direct imitation of our Lady.[39]

As might be expected, these victories on behalf of the Queen

of Virgins and her divine Son were not allowed to pass un-
challenged, and when Romans of high rank were also won over
to the life of evangelical perfection, the general undercurrent
of dissatisfaction was soon increased to fever-pitch. The critics
did not wish to abandon their religion entirely, but rather to
convince both themselves and society that it was possible to
get to heaven without the inconvenience of penance or the cross
of Christ. In short, this was the beginning of the first major
revolt of natural goodness against the folly of the Cross and the
dictates of supernatural faith concerning the necessity of actual
grace in everyday life. The controversy ended in the silencing
of the three ring-leaders (Helvidius, Jovinian and Vigilantius)
by St. Jerome and St. Ambrose; and then five years later, on
20 August 410, Rome was taken by Alaric the Hun and utterly
devastated. According to Pourrat quoting Palladius, "only those
were really saved who had carried their asceticism to the point
of flying from Rome into the desert in order to live there as
monks".[40]

In Gaul, meantime, small communities of monks had begun
to appear, also ascetics living in their own homes. The anchorite
system as such was unsuited to the climate and prevailing
political conditions. The work of St. Martin of Tours, St.
Honoratus of Arles and John Cassian was of particular significance,[41] and we also find great stress being laid on the importance
of meditation on the Scriptures. In Spain, on the other hand,
most of the monasteries were for women, and these were founded
by the Priscillianists, exaggerated ascetics who condemned
marriage and the use of meat.

From the sixth century onwards, the monastic rules in the
West began to multiply steadily, and the spirituality of this era
is associated almost entirely with these developments. There
were, however, no religious congregations or other forms of
monastic inter-government at this time. The general principles

of religious life were agreed upon by all, but each individual superior had his own views as to how the life of his monks should be organized, and he was not prepared to brook interference from his neighbours. Most famous of the rules was that of St. Benedict of Nursia in the early sixth century, this being based to a large extent on the earlier rules of St. Pachomius and St. Basil, on the Institutions and Conferences of Cassian, and on the famous Letter CCXI of St. Augustine to the religious women of Hippo. Also in Italy, but independently of St. Benedict, Abbot Paul and Abbot Stephen drew up monastic rules based on ancient traditions, and these corresponded on many points with the Benedictine legislation. A detailed account of the developments in Gaul and its neighbouring territories is supplied by Pourrat, also concerning the Benedictine Rule in practice.[42] Reference will be made later to the reforms which took place in the ninth century.

Meantime, St. Gregory the Great (540–604) had founded six monasteries in Sicily, then one in Rome on the Coelian Hill to which he retired. Later he was made a cardinal, then nuncio to Constantinople, finally pope in 590 until his death. Apart from his famous homilies and sermons, his main work is contained in his *Dialogues* written during the years of his pontificate. Also his *Pastoral Rule*, designed for the interior formation of the clergy, is of exceptional beauty and inspiration. He was an ideal pastor of souls himself, and in many ways resembles St. Augustine, above all concerning the place in our interior life that Jesus Christ must occupy. Like St. Alphonsus too, in the centuries to come, he knew from long experience that prayer alone can obtain the graces needed for sacerdotal perfection.

---

[1]Pourrat, *Christian Spirituality*, Vol. 1, p. 27. Cf. St. Thomas, *S.T.*, III, q. 62, art. 2.

[2]Pourrat, Vol. 1, p. 56.

[3]Ref. to St. Ignatius of Antioch, Ad Eph. x; see Pourrat, p. 57.

[4]Ref. to *Martyrdom of St. Polycarp*, ii, 2; see Pourrat, p. 57.

[5]Ep. ad Romanos; quoted by Pourrat, p. 58.

[6]Hom. XI in Lucam; quoted by Pourrat, p. 73.

[7]Scheeben, *Nature and Grace*, p. 10.

[8]Ref. to De quant. animae, n. 76; see Pourrat, p. 214.

[9]Ref. to *Confessions*, IX, 10; see Pourrat, p. 214.

[10]Ref. to De quant. animae, n. 76; see Pourrat, p. 214.

[11]Ref. to De temper. et virt. Cent. ii, 64; see Pourrat, p. 128.

[12]*Obscure Night of the Soul I*, 9.

[13]Cf. *Interior Castle*, Mansion 4, 3; also *Bk of Foundations*, 5 & 6.

[14]*Ascent of Mount Carmel*, II, 16—III, 15.

[15]Cf. St. John of the Cross, *Ascent II*, 26, 5–8.

[16]Cf. Farges, *Mystical Phenomena*, pp. 286–7.

[17]See, for example, *De Veritate*, q.18, art. 1. Cf. Farges, óp. cit., pp. 67–72, 79–80, 93–4, 258–65, 614–8, 631.

[18]Pourrat, Vol. 1, pp. 80–8.

[19]Pourrat, Vol. 1, pp. 88–100.

[20]Ref. to *Lausiac History;* see Pourrat, p. 120.

[21]Ref. to *Vita Antonii*, 4; see Pourrat, p. 112.

[22]*Vita Antonii*, 17; quoted by Pourrat, p. 135.

[23]Ref. to Cassian, *Collatio*, ix, 4; see Pourrat, p. 124.

[24]See Pourrat, Vol. 1, pp. 101–35.

[25]Ref. to *Ladder of Paradise*, Step 30; see Pourrat, p. 293.

[26]Loc. cit.

[27]See Pourrat, Vol. 1, p. 297.

[28]Pourrat, Vol. 1, p. 298.

[29]Ref. to *Mystagogia*, cap. I; see Pourrat, p. 299.

[30]Cf. Scheeben, *Nature and Grace*, p. 4.

[31]Pourrat, Vol. 1, p. 171.

[32]Pourrat, Vol. 1, p. 179.

[33]Pourrat, Vol. 1, pp. 185–207.

[34]Ref. to *De Ordine II*, n. 48; see Pourrat, p. 199.

[35]Pourrat, Vol. 1, p. 224.

[36]Pourrat, Vol. 1, p. 235.

[37]Ref. to De temper. et virt. Cent. I, 100; see Pourrat, p. 236.

[38]Hom. XI, In sanct. Mariam Deiparam; quoted by Pourrat, p. 238.

[39]See *De Virginibus II*, 6, 7, 15, 16.

[40]Ref. to *Lausiac History;* see Pourrat, p. 155.

[41]See Pourrat, Vol. 1, pp. 156–64.

[42]See Pourrat, Vol. 1, pp. 252–62; 243–51.

# MEDIAEVAL PANORAMA

## Foreword

WHEN WE look back over the first thousand years of the
Christian era and recall the different ways in which the influence
of the Word Incarnate came to be extended in the world, we
find that the greatest phenomenon by far is the dogmatic
authority of the Church together with the heroic witness of the
great popes and theological doctors when challenged by heresy.
Persecution and even martyrdom have served only to increase
within the Church her living consciousness of the truth deposited
in her safe-keeping, her consciousness of the mystery of the
hypostatic union, and God himself has raised up the saints
needed for her defence. All experiences of individual prayer
moreover, whether mystical or in accordance with ordinary
grace, can only be evaluated truly if seen against this background
of dogmatic truth; divorced from Christ and his Church, they
have no more permanence than soap-bubbles floating in the
sunlight, and they may even contain the germs of illuministic
falsehood. Similarly, our judgement of the men and women, who
have contributed most to the vast bulk of mystical literature
now extant, will always be more objective and consequently
more truthful if we regard their work in relation to the experience
of the Church as a whole. True mysticism is a gratuitous
*participation* in the God-consciousness of Christ's body on
earth; it is not a private possession and never can be.

Now the application of these Christo-centric principles to

our survey of mystical experience over the centuries gives us a refreshingly new angle of approach to the controversies so apt to arise over the relative greatness of the saints and the significance of their teaching. St. Augustine of Hippo, for example, might be despised by some because his known teaching does not embrace the particular theology of the Areopagite, similarly St. Athanasius, St. Cyril of Alexandria, St. Leo the Great, St. Gregory the Great, and all those mighty doctors whose intellects were as instruments for the Church during her periods of doctrinal affliction. The mystical theology of the Areopagite is indeed of the utmost importance, but its significance does not become fully apparent until much later on. Even in the teaching of St. Thomas Aquinas in the thirteenth century, its presence remains hidden from the eyes of many learned men, and the same is often true in regard to its place in the writings of St. Teresa and St. John of the Cross. Just as the stem and the leaves of a plant have to develop before the flowers, so here we must expect a gradual unfolding of the living organism that is the Church. Our next task, then, is to pursue the subject into the Middle Ages, and to note the gradual appearance of new elements in the spiritual picture as a whole. The development of religious life generally has most to do with the wider conceptions of the interior life which now become apparent.

## I   THE GREAT BENEDICTINE ABBOTS AND THEIR BACKGROUND

Many of the spiritual developments which actually took place during the Middle Ages, were foreseeable in the general trends of monastic life after the ninth century. Previous to that, the religious fervour of the monasteries in the West had been seriously undermined by the inauguration of a system of lay abbots and by the accumulation of too much wealth. St. Benedict of Aniane (751-821) had therefore been raised up by God to reform these abuses, also to bring every monastery in the Frankish empire under the single Benedictine Rule. A vow of stability was introduced to suppress the wanderings of discontented monks; serfs were admitted to the monasteries without restriction and on an equal footing with the others; a new emphasis was laid on the sanctifying power of Regular Observance; greater use was made of confession and Holy Communion; more time was devoted to the raising of intellectual standards; and greater devotion to our Lady was everywhere encouraged. Regular Observance combined with true evangelical poverty must necessarily encourage chastity and obedience, since otherwise the burden of these vows would be intolerable. Learning too, in particular a prayerful study of the Scriptures and the writings of the Fathers, brings both enlightenment to the intelligence and fervour to the will— yet not without a progressive diversity of opinion and the creation of doubt as to how far the mind of a monk should be modelled according to that of his superior. Is it a vice or is it a virtue for a man to think for himself, at any rate on speculative matters? This we shall find becomes the burning question in the West after the eleventh century. In the East, on the other hand, the monks for the most part were still taken up with corporal austerities, ecstatic contemplation, and the external problem of keeping the infidel Saracens at bay; so educational influences were far less marked.

After the tenth century in the West, a federation of Benedictine monasteries took place, so that henceforth they were grouped into *congregations* or *monastic orders*. The two principal congregations at that time were those of Cluny and Cîteaux, each having its own conception of the cloistered life and its underlying asceticism. By the twelfth century, no less than two thousand monasteries were in affiliation with Cluny, and although they did not produce any noteworthy spiritual writers, their influence for good was recognized throughout Europe. The personal holiness of the abbots and their love of discipline became well known; magnificent churches were built, and regular intellectual work began to be permitted. The monks of Cîteaux, on the other hand, maintained the utmost austerity— especially in regard to food, clothing, furnishings, and the part that manual labour should play in their daily life—and by the end of the twelfth century more than five hundred of their monasteries had come into existence. During the eleventh century, Benedictine discipline in Italy was restored on lines similar to that of the Cluniacs in France, the best-known reformers being: St. Romuald (1027), St. John Gualbert (1073), and St. Peter Damian (1072). St. Peter Damian considered that insufficient corporal chastisement was laid down in the rule, and he wrote several short works dealing with monastic questions. The Abbey of Notre-Dame du Bec in Normandy— made famous by the great St. Anselm from Piedmont (1033– 1109)—was founded by St. Herluin in the year 1034.

St. Anselm may be better known as an abbot of Bec or as an archbishop of Canterbury than as a mystic, yet the quality of his work places him in the forefront of spiritual writers and puts one in mind of St. Ambrose's commentary on Psalm cxviii:–

> The soul of the just is a kind of bride to the Word. If she longs for him, and yearns for him, and prays to him unceasingly, unquestioningly, stretching herself out to her uttermost extent to reach him, suddenly she will seem to hear his voice, though she sees him not, and deeply within her recognize the fragrance of his divinity: this, for the most part, is experienced by those who truly believe.[1]

St. Anselm was the first of the Benedictines to combine marked speculative and affective gifts. Reason, he considered, was a gift from God and should therefore be used in God's service, above all for the purpose of studying the faith and understanding its truths as far as possible. Thus in the first chapter of his *Proslogion* he exclaims with characteristic intensity: "I do not claim, Lord, to penetrate the depths of thy divine being, for I in no way feel my intelligence equal to the task; but I desire to understand something of thy truth which my heart believes and loves. I do not seek indeed to understand, in order to believe; but I believe in order to understand. For I am certain that unless I first believe, I shall not understand."[2] Again, in one of his works on the Trinity, he sets forth the following guiding principles: "The Christian has not the right to doubt what the Catholic Church believes with the heart and confesses with the mouth; but he should always, whilst firmly holding to this faith, loving it and living in conformity with it, seek what it is by his reason as far as he is capable of doing so. If he can understand, let him render thanks to God; if he cannot, let him be guarded from rising against it, but with head bowed down let him adore."[3] His devotion to our Lord's Passion and death on the Cross is very outstanding,[4] and amongst the prayers which he composed were several in honour of our Lady. The mystical symbolism which became so popular in the twelfth century did not appeal to him at all.

If St. Anselm was the outstanding Benedictine of the eleventh century, no less was St. Bernard of Clairvaux a hundred years later; yet scarcely could these two characters have been in greater contrast. Like St. John Climacus and the monks of the East, St. Bernard believed in the utmost rigour for the body, and he carried obedience to the point where no subject dared to retain his own will or opinion, since these he regarded as the "two leprosies which devour the hearts of monks".[5] On the positive side, however, he devoted much of his time to the study of sacred Scripture and meditation on the Psalms, thus ensuring for his monks a deep appreciation of the liturgy. The whole purpose of Benedictine piety is to feed the gift of divine love in the soul by this meditation on the mysteries of our Lord's earthly life, and St. Bernard insisted upon this especially when speaking of the qualities needed for the exercise of the priesthood.

Divine love and humility are regarded by St. Bernard as two aspects of the same mystery, but he is careful to distinguish between humility in relation to truth, and humility as a fruit of charity. The end must not be confounded with the means. A detailed and interesting account of this system of loving asceticism is provided by Pourrat.[6] Most striking of all, though, are St. Bernard's sermons for the Liturgical Year, especially his teaching concerning the healing effect on man's concupiscence of devotion to the sacred Infancy.[7] "This is not the time for us to proclaim the greatness and the glory of the Lord," he says, "for the Lord has made himself small and lovable beyond measure";[8] and again: "Let thy goodness, Lord, appear, so that man, created in thy image, may be able to imitate it; for we cannot imitate thy majesty, thy power or thy wisdom."[9] The beneficial influence of St. Bernard's sermons throughout the centuries is incalculable, possessing as they do such power and efficacy for good in the souls of others. While it is true that the mysticism arising from them is partly *sui generets*, the Church nonetheless has to feed the minds and hearts of her children at every stage of development, and we need not suppose that she could do this without making full use of the glorious diversity at her disposal.

The mystical theology of St. Bernard is contained chiefly in the sermons which he wrote on the Canticle of Canticles, and he was encouraged in this work by William, Abbot of St. Thierry near Rheims, who had been one of his disciples and who was to become his first biographer. Mystical love, for St. Bernard, may be *sensible*, *rational*, or *spiritual*, depending on the phase of development reached. Sensible love has for its object the Humanity of Jesus Christ and the mysteries of his mortal life; rational love is manifested when the mind becomes absorbed in the doctrines of faith concerning our Lord, to the exclusion of all error; and spiritual love occurs when God himself is the object of attention to the exclusion of all else. The Spiritual goal thus aimed at, seems to be identical with the perfect prayer of the Eastern school as exemplified by St. John Climacus. St. Bernard, however, elaborates on his own personal concept of the spiritual marriage to which he considers the soul should now aspire, and which he describes as a "veritable embrace" wherein "the identification of the two wills makes of the two minds one only same thing".[10] From simple affective contemplation, the bride is raised by ectasy to the presence of the King in the depths of her soul,[11] and there the divine kiss so long and ardently sought after is granted. In this, the essence of mystical experience is said to consist.[12] Such ecstasy, moreover, may be intensified to the point of rapture; and in this event, the activity of the mind under the influence of infused light may be so great that the vision of God, as if in a flash of lightning, is manifested. Normally, however, the experience is either associated with the contemplation of the truths of faith or else remains purely affective. St. Bernard seems to reject the possibility in this life of essential union (as granted to Moses and St. Paul), but he uses St. Paul's words about seeing "through a glass in a dark manner" (1 Cor. xiii.12) to describe his own peak experience. Further, he requires the presence of certain spiritual images, which he likens to the golden chains bedecking the bride in the Canticle of Canticles, and these he says are necessary for the mediation of divine Wisdom to the soul. Apparently these images may on occasion be perceptible to the senses—even although the gold is purely symbolic of the Divinity—but the angels, not the imagination, are responsible for suggesting these to the mind of the bride.[13] Thus the mystical heights for St. Bernard, no less than for St. Augustine, are clearly concerned with the *activity* of the mind under the influence of the divine light, and he says of this contemplative vision that it "does not startle, but calms; it does not over-excite through curiosity, but satisfies; it does not tire, but brings repose. It is quietude in a true sense".[14] Such an experience certainly indicates the gratuitous influence of the Holy Ghost, as distinct from the disturbing effects or emotional excitements so often produced by the devil when attempting to withdraw the soul from the safe path of humility and obedience, but it in no way describes the infused touches of union which characterize the last three mansions of St. Teresa. It has been suggested more than once by modern writers that St. Bernard's "spiritual images" might be the same as these substantial touches; but that, philosophically speaking, is impossible. Again, one associates the created action of the Holy Ghost with his sevenfold gifts, but one cannot describe these gifts as "spiritual images". The latter then, necessary though they may be for the perfection of mystical experience in the affective unitive way, are no less amongst the apprehensions to be rejected by the soul on the road to the highest summit of Mount Carmel. St. Bernard says, too, that mystical union—since it passes so quickly—leaves the soul with an unquenchable yearning for it to return; whereas, in the last three mansions of St. Teresa—although the infused touches are of even shorter duration—the ordinary *state* of contemplation within the soul is habitual. During the periods of interior affliction, it is true, this contemplation tends to be obscure and painful; but gradually it finds expression in the peaceful darkness of pure faith *which enables the soul to rejoice at all times*, as much in the divinity as in the humanity of Christ the Redeemer. If the soul in this state were to yearn for particular graces and infused consolations, instead of devoting its strength to the practical needs of others, according to its state in life, it would destroy very rapidly the delicate work of the Holy Ghost in preparing it for the highest apostolic ideal possible here on earth. In fact, during the next three centuries, Benedictine mysticism became progressively more visionary and prophetic in utterance, and much of it was illuministic, as in the case of Joachim of Flora who died in 1202. On the other hand, genuine saints were raised up such as St. Hildegarde, St. Elizabeth of Schoenau, St. Gertrude, St. Mechtilde, and St. Mechtilde of Magdeburg in Germany, also St. Bridget in Sweden, and devotion to the Sacred Heart of Jesus received tremendous impetus during this time. The devotion of St. Bernard to our Lady, to St. Joseph and to the Guardian Angels is well known, and is described in detail by Pourrat.[15]

William of St. Thierry, who has been mentioned already in connexion with St. Bernard, makes a distinctive contribution to spiritual theology in that he draws attention to the *memoria* of the soul, the source of the two spiritual faculties, understanding and will. This word *memoria*, in Cistercian usage, means a great deal more than what is connotated by the English word "memory". Thus, in the mind of St. Bernard, *memoria* refers to the soul's *active* power of recalling knowledge, in particular however *the knowledge of Christ's Passion* by means of which the soul is raised to mystical contemplation; and then, in the mind of William of St. Thierry, it denotes that *habitual recollection of God* which is implanted in the depths of every soul, even although obscured by the darkness of sin, and which comes under the influence of infused hope. Blosius was later to say that "we ourselves, in this inner sanctuary of the soul in which the divine image lies hid, are like unto God";[16] and he explains too that in the enkindled illumination of mystical union, "the Father (manifests himself) in the memory, by the simple line of thought; the Son in the intellect, by clear knowledge; the

Holy Ghost in the will, by ardent love".[17] This emphasis on the *memoria* in the second sense of the term—a usage which derives from St. Augustine[18]—is found more commonly in the Eastern Church, also in the minds of such modern theologians as Matthias Scheeben, and it explains for example what Julius Tyciak means when he writes: "In hope, the soul shares the Father's infinite consciousness of himself and of his power. Hope is a repose in God, a being clasped by God"—God the Father, that is to say—"the source of all life, all power, all glory."[19]

## 2 THE TWELFTH-CENTURY IDEALISTS

St. Bernard had no time for intellectual theories, and appreciated only what to him seemed practical or directly associated with the problem of man's salvation. Citing the apostles as our example in this respect, he used to say: "They are our masters, they have deeply learned from the Sovereign Master the ways of life, and these they have taught us until today. . . . They have not taught us to read Plato, nor to unravel the subtleties of Aristotle. They have not taught us how to study without ever arriving at the knowledge of truth. They have taught us to live. And think you that to know how to live is little knowledge? Christ did not draw his apostles from the schools of rhetoricians and philosophers."[20] Even nowadays St. Bernard's argument is sometimes quoted in support of the idea that it is a waste of time and money to build Catholic schools. He was, however, wise in insisting that the pursuit of knowledge should never become an end in itself. As Scheeben writes in the *Mysteries of Christianity:*—

> Reason must strive more to promote the development of faith than its own good, since the object of faith is immeasurably

nobler and more worthy than its own proper object, and comprises everything that reason longed for by nature but could not reach by its own efforts. Therefore reason must place its natural concepts at the disposal of faith, and must endeavour to elucidate the objects of faith according to the norm of revelation by determining to what extent such concepts can be analogously applied to them;[21]

again:

Like the nuptials of nature with grace, the yoking of reason with faith in the theological sphere has its fairest and most sublime ideal in the espousals . . . of the Virgin of virgins with the Holy Spirit, whereby she became the Mother of him who is personal Wisdom incarnate.[22]

These two quotations help to redress the balance in the interests of speculative spirituality.

In the eleventh century, as already noted, St. Anselm was the first of the great scholastics. In the twelfth century, Peter Abelard was the outstanding figure, and then followed St. Thomas Aquinas together with many other scholastic theologians. Peter Abelard, as might be expected, came in for the brunt of the opposition from the Benedictine school; but this, in part at least, was due to his own natural impatience and forthright ways of expressing himself. William of St. Thierry became his principal opponent, and it was due to the influence of William of St. Thierry that St. Bernard wrote to one of the cardinals in Rome in the following strain: "Master Abelard exceeds the limits set by our fathers. Disputing and writing on matters of faith, the Sacraments, and the blessed Trinity, he changes all at will, adds or minimizes as it pleases him. . . . There is nothing in heaven or earth that he does not know unless it be himself."[23] The Benedictine opposition was certainly powerful, but it was not stronger than life itself, and in the course of the twelfth century the new school of St. Victor sought in the

4

idealism of Plato to find a suitable balance between the two extremes of affective and rational thinking.

The Abbey of St. Victor in Paris had been founded about the year 1108 by William of Champeaux, a friend of St. Bernard's and a former professor at Notre-Dame de Paris. Observance was almost as severe as in the Cistercian life, except that the greater part of the day was devoted to study rather than to manual labour, but the actual rule was based on that of the Canons of St. Augustine. Unlike the Premonstratensians, who had been founded on similar lines by St. Norbert of Xanten about the year 1120, the Victorines did not undertake parish duties but gave themselves up to the pursuit of philosophy and mystical contemplation. The main representatives of this school were: Hugh (d. 1140); Richard (d. 1173); and Adam (d. 1177). Hugh, in particular, was strongly sympathetic towards the new speculative trends.

Victorine mysticism is based on a symbolistic conception of the universe and professes to embrace truth as a whole, beginning at a natural or scientific level, progressing by means of intuitive meditation, and finally arriving at the mystical realities which lie hidden beneath the veils of material creation. No clear distinction is made between the natural and the supernatural, between the object of philosophy and the object of faith, and the contemplation of revealed truth is regarded as a continuation or perfecting of the natural truths already comprehended. The rôle of grace is not denied, but the word "mystical" in the Victorine sense means "symbolic" or "affective"; also every branch of science is claimed to be religious, since everything to do with creation tells man about God and the whole universe has been restored by Christ. Such an outlook, which often contains a subtle form of intellectual pelagianism, has been expressed in modern times by the late Teilhard de Chardin, S.J., in *Le Milieu Divin*, but it has its origin in the third-century school of Alexandria, that is to say, in the time of Clement and Origen. Certainly there is much of interest in the symbolistic approach to creation,[24] but there is plenty of scope as well for imagination, exaggeration, and even detriment to true faith, accounting no doubt for the disapproval of such theologians as St. Anselm and William of St. Thierry.

The teaching of the Victorines, as regards mystical contemplation and ecstasy, has been synthetized by Richard of St. Victor. We must remember, however, that no distinction is made between the domains of philosophy and theology. Mysticism was claimed to be the term of all knowledge, science the doorway to love. Contemplation was thus defined as "a clear insight into truth, accompanied by lively sentiments of joy which the perception of the beauty of this truth brings to the soul",[25] but with many subjective variations on the theme which Pourrat describes in detail.[26]

The fifth and sixth of Richard's degrees of contemplation are the ones we are principally concerned with here, and these are explained in Richard's best-known book *Benjamin Major*. Raised to these mystical heights, "we come to know, through divine revelation, truth which no human reason can fully understand and no reasoning can enable us to discover with certainty".[27] Fifth-degree truths exceed the comprehension of our reason, sixth-degree truths—as, for example, the mystery of the Trinity—even seem to be opposed to our reason. In this however, we are aided by the divine light, to obtain which we have first to strive for moral perfection. Richard admits that all favours in the ecstatic order are supernatural and gratuitous, but he sees no reason why we should not desire them, and hold ourselves in readiness to receive them if God so wills. Being strictly ecstatic, all such contemplation is characterized by a combination of infused light and infused knowledge, the latter sometimes being prophetic in character. The possibility of pure essential vision (as in the case of Moses and St. Paul) is also claimed, but Richard admits that the grace of exalted contemplation is very uncertain. Unlike St. Bernard, he did not require mirrors (infused expressed species) for the contemplation of God, but held that this takes place directly, no mediation being required. This was considered to be in the tradition both of St. Augustine and of the Areopagite, but certainly it bears no resemblance whatever to the Dionysian contemplation which takes place through infused impressed species.[28]

For Richard, then, ecstasy consisted of three degrees of interior alienation from ordinary consciousness: first, a suspension of the bodily senses; then the suspension of the imagination; then the overwhelming of the intelligence by divine light: and this experience, which is always associated with degrees of personal intensity, might be precipitated by love or by admiration or by joy. "Intense love," he said, "produces ecstasy when the soul is so enkindled with the fire of heavenly desire that the flame of divine love, growing within it in an unusual way, liquefies it like wax, renders it light like smoke and causes it to rise to the heavenly regions."[29] Richard claimed, too, that some ecstatics could produce these effects almost at will.[30] It is not surprising, therefore, that much heterodox mysticism occurred during the twelfth century, including the claim to impeccability and to infallibility of inspiration once perfect union with God had been attained; but at least these errors have served a purpose from the point of view of warning future generations of interior souls.

### 3   St. Thomas Aquinas and the Flowering of Speculative Spirituality

During the thirteenth century, the scholastic method created by St. Anselm and so vigorously pursued by Peter Abelard began to assume a practical importance hitherto unsuspected. We have seen in the preceding paragraphs how the platonic philosophy of the Victorine school assisted in the development of speculative theology, but this in fact gave place almost entirely to the philosophy of Aristotle as interpreted by St. Albert the Great and St. Thomas Aquinas. The occasion for this tremendous intellectual advance came about through the influence of Siger de Brabant, thirteenth-century champion of the Arabian intellectual system known as Averroism.

Averroes, who was born in Cordova in 1128 and died in Morocco at the age of seventy, had been a famous physician and philosopher. He had taught that in all mankind there is only one intellect, and in attacking both the Christian and Jewish religions, he had endeavoured to interpret Aristotle for his own ends. Siger de Brabant did the same thing, and it thus became a matter of urgency to show that Aristotle was potentially on the side of orthodoxy.

Philosophy, of course, provides no more than a substructure for mysticism, be the experience Christian or otherwise; but it was customary for the scholastic theologians to incorporate their views on spirituality with the rest of their writings, and for this reason—in the case of St. Thomas especially—it is easy to overlook some of the deeper aspects of teaching about mystical prayer. Peter Lombard, writing in the twelfth century, had adopted the views of Peter Abelard in order to perfect them, and in the third book of his *Sentences* we find a considerable amount of teaching about the theological virtues and cardinal virtues, the gifts of the Holy Ghost, and the principles governing the interior life. William of Auvergne, Bishop of Paris (1249), another of the creators of scholastic theology, wrote in a similar style. The teaching of St. Thomas Aquinas (1225–74) is so extensive that we cannot do more than indicate the points bearing special reference to our subject of enquiry. A more detailed synopsis is already provided by Pourrat.[31]

Before all else, St. Thomas stresses the rôle of divine grace as the principle of our supernatural interior life. The Christian, by means of his natural faculties, acts as man; but by grace, which is a sharing in the nature of God himself, he performs acts meritorious of the eternal reward to which he is called through Baptism. Grace itself is not a substance, but it has the power to adhere to the soul's natural substance in such a way that it permeates the whole. From the same grace, too, are derived the theological virtues together with the gifts of the Holy Ghost, also the cardinal virtues and the many other infused moral virtues dependent on them. For each and every supernatural *act*, however, the special help or impulse of God is required; hence the important distinction—which is sometimes overlooked—between habitual grace and actual grace. The influence of the infused virtues alone, always leaves the soul under the control of reason and faith; but the sevenfold gifts, on the other hand, tend progressively to bring the soul under the direct mastery of the Holy Ghost—in proportion, that is, as pure faith assumes the initiative of reason. The teaching of St. Thomas concerning the relationship between the gifts and the theological virtues[32] is of great importance to the proper understanding of Christian mysticism.

Following the teaching of the New Testament and of St. Augustine, St. Thomas thinks of Christian perfection in terms of charity, that supernatural virtue by which we love God above all things and our neighbour as ourselves for God's sake. The other infused virtues tend to perfection in proportion as they contribute to the intensification of charity; but charity itself is the principle of *unity* between the soul and God, and therefore possesses a perfection all its own. Like St. Augustine, too, St. Thomas makes a distinction between absolute perfection and relative perfection, only the latter being possible during this earthly pilgrimage. Thus charity may be declared perfect in a man who "gives his whole heart to God habitually", that is to say "by neither thinking nor desiring anything contrary to the love of God".[33] St. Thomas, moreover, regards devotion (which is part of the virtue of religion) as a most necessary adjunct to the practice of charity, and he defines it as "the will to give oneself readily to things concerning the service of God".[34] Above all, then, charity here below is *progressive* and closely associated with the generosity of the soul concerned.

As regards the perfection of charity inspired by the counsels of perfection, St. Thomas says that this consists in the renunciation of temporal goods as far as possible, "even such as are lawful, because they occupy the mind and hinder the actual movement of the heart towards God".[35] It is by "inward spiritual growth" that the soul attains to "the state of perfection in relation to the divine judgement", and this explains why "nothing hinders some from being perfect without being in the state of perfection, and some in the state of perfection without being perfect".[36] In this same part of the *Summa*,[37] St. Thomas also discusses the respective claims of manual labour and of study in the monastic life.

In St. Thomas's treatise on the virtues, moral theology and spiritual theology are closely mingled.[38] Already in the twelfth century, Hugh of St. Victor had attempted to draw up a genealogical tree distinguishing the fruits of the flesh from those of the spirit,[39] but St. Thomas's brilliant new classification soon caused this earlier attempt to be forgotten, and it also inspired much of the carving of the sculptors of the age. As regards meditation, too, St. Thomas did not fully endorse the Victorine view-point, but restricted the scope of supernatural meditation to "the consideration of such things as are of a nature to awaken our love of God".[40] He explained the theological background to prayer[41] but without adding anything of consequence to this present study.

The teaching of St. Thomas about temptation and how to master the passions is in marked contrast with the pessimism of St. Augustine, as indeed with Eastern asceticism generally, and lays the foundation for a totally new approach in the field of spiritual direction. For St. Thomas, the source of every sin is the *inordinate* love of self; but the love of self, being part of the nature of man as the affective side of him, is not necessarily inordinate. Its natural inclination towards that which is good, be this the good of the body or of the soul, constitutes concupiscence in the philosophical sense of the word only; and thus our delectable appetite should always be distinguished from its irascible or concupiscible counterparts whence arise the passions. From the concupiscible appetite are born the passions which urge on the soul towards the object of its desire; from the irascible appetite come those which pit themselves against the obstacles standing in the way of the desired possession. These two appetites are closely related, but they can only be reduced to a single source in the sense that "all the passions are caused by love".[42] St. Thomas gives the six passions of the concupiscible appetite as: love and hatred, desire and aversion, joy and sadness; then the five passions of the irascible appetite as: hope and despair, fear, daring and anger.[43] In themselves, these passions are neither good nor bad, but only in proportion as they "accord or disaccord with reason".[44] The stoics, as we have seen, tried to eliminate all passion as an evil in itself. St. Augustine realized that such elimination was impossible, but attributed the fact to original sin, to the inherent weakness of man; and St. Bernard tried to consume it in the fires of divine love. St. Thomas, on the other hand, whilst recognizing the value of wise discipline and self-denial as a means of helping to maintain order in the soul, was the first to point out that evil lies only in *disorder*, and the same is true of the Christ-centred asceticism of St. John of the Cross. Control, not repression, is the real secret of interior liberty.

In preparing the mind for the contemplative life, St. Thomas stresses the importance of reading and meditation, of consideration and prayer. Moral stability is also necessary, since otherwise the soul will lack the application required for the contemplation of divine things. As Pourrat says, "St. Thomas is very precise as to the object of contemplation. It is divine truth revealed and known by faith, to the exclusion of scientific truth discovered by reason"; but the contemplative ordinarily "is not able to perceive the divine essence itself".[45]

In contemplation, then, the soul is brought to the consideration of God as he really is, but there are only two ways in which the immediate vision of the divine essence becomes possible. The first is through the miraculous type of rapture as granted to St. Paul, and the second is through an infused impressed species substantially received. "That which the contemplative perceives is not God himself, seen directly," Pourrat says, "but a sign, a 'created effect' of a supernatural order, by which God becomes known."[46] Pourrat, however, then proceeds to equate this "created effect" with the infused *expressed* species required by St. Bernard for the perfection of mediate contemplation as experienced in the affective unitive way—an error in synthesis rendering the whole subject inexplicable. The "created effect" referred to by St. Thomas[47] is identical with the *patiens divina* of St. Dionysius, again with terms *illapsus* and "substantial touch," the only mediation involved being that provided (as in every created grace) by Jesus and Mary. This divine action is suffered directly by the substance of the soul, and in this way the divine essence is said to be "touched", "tasted", "smelt", "heard" or "seen", according to whichever spiritual sense carries to the perceiving intellect *a reflex knowledge* of what has occurred. This is the essential experience of the last three mansions of St. Teresa, and although it is characterized by progressive degrees of clarity and conviction, one must insist that it is different *in kind* from the contemplation of the affective unitive way. Here, both Agent and patient are united in the single common action, and this unique phenomenon can only take place at substantial level, totally beyond the reach of angels and devils and even of one's own imagination. The infused *expressed* species required by St. Bernard, on the other hand, are given directly to the understanding (even if not to the imagination), after which the soul proceeds to its act of contemplation. In short, then, "the ultimate perfection of the human intellect is the divine truth: and other truths perfect the intellect in relation to the divine truth".[48]

Rapture, St. Thomas teaches, is a phenomenon "whereby a man is uplifted by the Spirit of God to things supernatural and withdrawn from his senses".[49] It differs from ecstasy in that "a certain violence is experienced".[50] Further, he explains that "without being withdrawn from his senses" it is impossible for man "to see God in his essence";[51] and that is why "Paul's vision, while he was in rapture, was like the vision of the blessed ... as to the thing seen, and unlike ... as to the mode of seeing, because he saw not so perfectly as do the saints in heaven".[52] In other words, his participation in the light of glory was only momentary and in the nature of prophetic grace. Such an experience, moreover, is in no way essential to the normal mystical journey of the soul towards transforming union in the Teresian sense of the term, and it is extremely dangerous to try to induce it.

## 4    THE FRANCISCAN SCHOOL OF SERAPHIC LOVE

The teaching of St. Thomas about charity and perfection is usually regarded as fundamental to the Christian view of spirituality; but of no less importance is his exposition of charity's practical relations with faith and hope.[53] Further, he stresses the vital point that the intellect cannot be purified by the virtues pertaining to the appetitive power;[54] only faith can effect this cleansing of the cognoscitive eye. Even the souls in purgatory are perfect in charity, yet their spiritual sight requires greater refinement before becoming capable of the beatific vision. Here below, then, faith and hope are the principal agents of purification for the intellect and memory, and although all genuine contemplatives are ready to acknowledge the need for this refining process, marked differences of opinion exist as to how these virtues should be exercised. This, in fact, accounts for most of the diversity in the expression of mystical truth: as we are, so does God offer us his sanctifying help.

In the case of St. Francis of Assisi, the two qualities most outstanding may be described as: a transfiguring spirit of *joy*, born of his deep compassion for the sufferings of the Crucified; and a supernatural *simplicity*, born of the gift of knowledge which operated unceasingly in his mind and heart, bringing with it the connatural fruits of wisdom, chastity and peace in so eminent a degree. If we examine these qualities more closely, we shall acquire a truer understanding of his other well-known characteristics, avoiding above all the sentimental view of his devotion to birds and animals.

Every interior soul in love with Jesus Christ forms an individual concept of the Sacred Humanity, and when certain aspects of the Sacred Humanity occupy a predominant position in that concept, all else tends to become subordinated to the pursuit or imitation of the central attraction. With St. Francis, then, the fact that he had even less time than St. Bernard for speculation and book-learning, and despised material security almost to the point of fanaticism, meant only that his own attention was otherwise engaged. On the one hand, his heart was captivated by the absolute poverty of Jesus Christ and the humiliation of his sufferings for our sake; on the other hand, his mind had the whole book of creation upon which to feast, and in this the gift of knowledge gave him the power of essential penetration to an extraordinary degree. Thus Thomas of Celano, who was his principal biographer, tells us that some two years before his death, whilst praying one morning on the slopes of Mount Alvernia, "he was uplifted to God by desire and by seraphic ardour and felt himself transformed by a tender compassion for him who, in the excess of his charity, willed to be crucified. . . . A wonderful ardour of love rested in Francis's soul; and, more wonderful still, in his body there appeared the impression of the stigmata of our Lord Jesus Christ".[55] The intense delight which he took in all the living creatures of God was in no way based on the symbolism of the Victorines, but was an immediate effect of the infused gift of knowledge. He resembled, too, the monks of the East in his views on obedience. One way or the other, the virtue of faith in a religious needs continual exercise.

As the number of Friars Minor increased, it became correspondingly difficult to reconcile literal poverty with the need to establish monasteries, and after the death of St. Francis in 1226 sharp controversies arose over the practical interpretation of his spirit. Up to the year 1257, the extremists found a leader in John of Parma. Then came the election of St. Bonaventure as Minister-General, an office which he held until he was made Cardinal and Bishop of Alabano in 1273, the year before his death.

Although trained in Paris as a theologian, St. Bonaventure felt no great attraction for the philosophy of Aristotle as interpreted by the great Dominicans of the time. Intellectually, he preferred the teaching of Plato; but he was always predominantly affective in his spiritual outlook, and for that reason he was strongly drawn to the writings of St. Bernard. Thus he is well known for his devotion to the Blessed Trinity, but he always thought of heavenly beatitude in terms of the will. In his devotion to our Lord's Passion, he closely resembled St. Francis, for he meditated unceasingly on the sorrows of the Crucified and exhorted all Christians to do likewise.

St. Bonaventure was probably the first theologian to divide the spiritual life into three recognized stages: that of purgation, that of illumination, and finally that of union with God by charity. Security and tranquillity mark the top of his mystical ladder, sweetness and fervour the beginning. Ecstasy is liable to be caused by the intensity of love, leading to a kind of mystical sleep akin to the apatheia of St. John Climacus. St. Bonaventure himself does not describe ecstasy, but he refers to the experiences of St. Francis of Assisi. Of greater interest are his dogmatic writings about the mystery of the Blessed Trinity and the mystery of the Hypostatic Union.[56]

Towards the end of the fourteenth century, the Friars Minor were divided officially into "Observants" and "Conventuals", the former being related to the earlier followers of John of Parma but freed from heretical tendencies. During the next two centuries, further divisions were made. Among the Franciscan nuns, St. Clare and her companions had been the contemporaries of St. Francis himself; then St. Colette (1447) became the equivalent of St. Teresa as regards the reform of the Friars Minor in France. The religious life of Blessed Angela of Foligno (d. 1309) was filled with ecstasies and visions of an intellectual nature, also for twelve years she was sustained without nourishment other than the Blessed Sacrament. Pourrat assembles the following features as characteristic of the mystical union described in her writings: first, the identification of the human will with that of God; secondly, "an unction which suddenly renews the soul and which renders all the members of the body docile and submissive to it", so that "no trouble can then approach it, and there is certainty that God is there and that he speaks";[57] thirdly, the ineffable "embrace" wherein "Jesus presses the soul to himself (*stringit ad se animam rationalem*)".[58] Closely parallel with this type of spirituality were the mystical experiences of the Ven. Ana Maria de San José (1581–1632), abbess of the Discalced Franciscans in Salamanca, whose autobiography was first published in 1665. In the case of St. Catherine of Bologna (1413–63), her struggles and liberating ecstasies were as extraordinary as the trials which beset her entire religious life. Even the day of her death—9th March 1463— was revealed to her in ecstasy. Many souls were helped through reading of the struggles which she had described during her lifetime, also of the heavenly graces which had sustained her human frailty. Strange as these experiences may seem to the twentieth-century mind, one has to accept the fact—at least in the case of the canonized saints—that genuine mystical grace may be manifested, through the power of God, in many astonishing ways. It is a different matter when extraordinary phenomena are desired and esteemed for their own sake.

## 5   THE CONNATURAL AFFECTIVITY OF THE DOMINICAN SCHOOL

The work of the Dominican order has already been mentioned briefly in connexion with St. Thomas Aquinas and his predecessor St. Albert the Great. So far, however, the chief reference has been to the mystical doctrine of St. Thomas in its distinctive aspects, that is to say, his teaching about the "angelic mode" of contemplation. In contrast with this, the Dominican school as such seems to identify itself more particularly with the affective contemplation of the simple unitive way, a form of contemplation explainable in terms of the connaturality of the spiritual powers and of the ordinary rôle of the gifts in bringing the Christian soul to the perfection of charity. Important as these fundamental points are, and always will be, they fail to do justice to the full genius of St. Thomas.

St. Dominic himself (1170–1221) was a close friend of St. Francis of Assisi, and many points of resemblance exist between the two orders. St. Dominic however wished his Friars Preacher to be as learned as possible, and he based their monastic life on the Rule of St. Augustine. Fundamentally they were to be Canons Regular, but with the further dignity of consecration to the work of the apostolate. St. Dominic was a preacher of tremendous fire and apostolic zeal, Spanish by birth, ascetic by nature, and a great man of prayer. He effected miracles even in his lifetime, and like St. Francis of Assisi was an ecstatic. St. Vincent Ferrer of Valencia (1357–1419) was of a similar spiritual temperament.

In Italy, the inspiration of St. Dominic found expression initially in the work of painters and sculptors, above all in the master-touch of Fra Angelico of Fiesole (1387–1455), whose every work had been conceived in prayer. Then the life and social mission of St. Catherine of Siena (1347–80) is also noteworthy, for in this she resembled the prophetic St. Hildegarde of Germany and St. Bridget of Sweden.

The life of St. Catherine of Siena, as Pourrat observes, "was one long series of extraordinary mystical experiences",[59] and these are well known to all who have read her various biographies. Most likely, they were necessary on account of her reforming apostolate and the influence within the Church which she was called upon to exercise. Paradoxically, though, two of St. Catherine's most outstanding characteristics were her humility and her self-knowledge, especially in regard to the dangers of spiritual pride and spiritual self-will. For mystical union, she required the sense of the divine presence within the soul, but there is no clear indication that this infused experience exceeded the limits of connatural affectivity. In the *Dialogue*, for example, our Lord says of the souls perfected in love: "I remain with them uninterruptedly by my grace and by the experience which I give them of my presence. As soon as they are willing to unite the mind to me by a sense of love, they may do so, because their desire has reached so great a union with me through the sense of love that nothing in the world can part it. . . . These most perfect souls never lose the sense of my presence within them."[60] Although given to ecstasy in outstanding degree, St. Catherine makes no claim to any vision of the divine essence. The theological views which she expresses are closely modelled on those of St. Thomas Aquinas.

In Germany during the fourteenth century, there were various Dominican writers and mystics, and Pourrat in his sketch of the Rhineland[61] draws special attention to the contemporary religious associations which constitute their background. These associations were mainly connected with:

The Beghards and their feminine equivalent the Beguines, both from the Low Countries;

The Brethren of the Free Spirit, who exercised a gravely heretical influence—over the Beghards and Beguines in particular—fostering the spread of immorality, pantheism and even Averroism;

The Friends of God, who gave themselves up to the rigours of asceticism and practised absolute detachment from all things, though not without illuministic tendencies and reluctance to accept ecclesiastical discipline. Both John Tauler and Henry Suso had frequent dealings with them.

The above-mentioned writers and mystics of the German Dominican school include the following:

Meister Eckhart (1260–1329), who was regarded as the founder of the German mystical school. His teaching, which was obscure even at best, appears to have been influenced by the pantheism of the Brethren of the Free Spirit, and twenty-eight propositions drawn from his works were condemned by Pope John XXII in the year 1331.

John Tauler (1290–1361 approx.), who preached mostly in the orthodox Beguinages. Much of his teaching was later champ-ioned by Blosius, the Benedictine Abbot of Liessies in Belgium, but by many it has been misinterpreted. Blosius gives an admirable summary of the essential points in the two append-ices published at the end of his own *Book of Spiritual Instruc-tion*, and the devotion of Tauler to our Lady is especially noteworthy.

Blessed Henry Suso (1295–1365), who was an ecstatic, consumed by his special devotion to the Eternal Wisdom with whom he contracted a spiritual marriage. Both his austerities and his moral sufferings were extraordinary, but they did not quench the fire of his love or his zeal to make reparation for the general condition of the Church in the fourteenth century. He was beatified by Pope Gregory XVI on 16th April 1831.

Nicholas of Strasbourg, who came to be associated with the German mystical school in the fourteenth century, also with various German Dominican nuns whose experiences were of the spectacular order.

Examples of the teaching of Tauler and Suso are included in the next section. Fuller biographical details are already given by Pourrat in the last part of his chapter on the Dominican school.[62]

## 6  THE ESSENTIAL MYSTICISM OF THE GERMAN SCHOOL

The great preoccupation of the German mystical writers in the

5

fourteenth century was the unity of God, and how best to
prepare the soul to lose itself in this sea of the divine perfections.
Mystical union, as they conceived it, took place in the essence
of the soul. That was the first point. Secondly, it eliminated
all idea of mediation between the soul and God. Thirdly, it
sought to suppress the difference between the soul and God. In
order to comprehend this strange point of view, one has to
study at some length the respective doctrines of Ruysbroeck,
Tauler and Suso.[63]

Blessed Jan van Ruysbroeck, as distinct from the other two
mentioned, was a Canon Regular of St. Augustine and Flemish
by birth. His outlook, however, was in most ways akin
to that of the German school, and while still a young priest
in Brussels he began to write against the Brethren of the Free
Spirit and their heretical teachings. Some twelve of his treatises
have been preserved and bear many resemblances to those of
Tauler.

The Rhenish mystics taught in the first place that a solid
foundation of penance and mortification and ordinary moral
virtue must be established, but that the soul—after acquiring
this basic stability—should then reach out to a perfect renunciation of self in all things, even in regard to what is lawful. The
gifts of fear, piety and knowledge, Tauler said, " prepare man for
a sublime and true perfection"; but the gifts of counsel, fortitude,
wisdom and understanding "finish it inwardly and outwardly,
and prepare it for the highest end, that state of most pure,
most glorious and true perfection",[64] namely essential union
with God. It should be clear then that this extreme renunciation,
inspired as it is by the gifts of counsel and fortitude, was not
originally intended for all men, but only for those with the
necessary ascetical grounding and vocation from the Holy
Ghost. This granted, no further qualification is needed for the
dictum of Tauler that this detachment is meant to extend to every

circumstance of our earthly life.[65] This point was also made when discussing the doctrine of the Areopagite.

Most distressing yet sanctifying of all, is the state of abandonment in which God sometimes leaves the soul for long or short periods. In this condition, as Tauler says, "man is left entirely to his own strength, so that he no longer knows anything, either of the graces and consolations of God, or of all that he had formerly acquired. All that is taken from him, so that he no longer knows which way to turn or where to go. . . . Man is here deprived of himself, left in complete abandonment. He is swallowed up in the depth of the divine will."[66] The sufferings inherent in this painful trial should, of course, be united with those of the Crucified.[67]

After we have reached the supreme degree of renunciation, Ruysbroeck (like Tauler) believes that "we resign, through love, our will and all that belongs to us to the free will of God" in such a way that this will is "freely taken and cloistered by love in the will of God without return".[68] As regards the concomitant banishing of all images and sensible representations from the mind,[69] however, Tauler cautions that a high degree of interior perfection must first be achieved, and he insists that it would be harmful to try to anticipate the grace of adhering to God by means of the naked intelligence.[70]

As already stressed in the first part of this study, the state of interior ligature or apparent emptiness of the mind is produced for the most part by the direct action of God within the soul; the work of renouncing all particular consolations, visions, raptures, dreams, locutions and the like, is no more than complementary to the interior stripping which God himself effects through the infused light of faith. God as he really is surpasses infinitely all our human conceptions, and that is why the intelligence can never truly know him whilst making use of forms and images. Only when this ordinary activity is replaced,

supernaturally and gratuitously, by the divine action is it possible
for mystical union to be effected substantially. Such is that
blessed state of mind which Tauler calls "the divine darkness . . .
the delightful state in which all forms and all images are silent".[71]
Pourrat observes that whereas mystical contemplation for the
German writers is "a state of almost complete passiveness", the
experience of ecstatics such as St. Catherine of Siena would seem
rather to betoken a "superactivity of mind" whilst raised to the
mystic state.[72] This, however, need not surprise us, since the
experience of ecstasy does not pertain to substantial union, but
affects the rational soul directly. From this point of view, it is
a less perfect form of union than that of St. Dionysius, allowing
however for the exceptional and miraculous alienation from the
senses which enabled St. Paul to glimpse the uncreated essence
of God.

At the root of the German doctrine, as already remarked, is
one simple idea having its origin in neoplatonic thought: we
come from God by creation, we return to him by contemplation:
and although this is not really meant in any pantheistic sense, the
German mystics are none too clear in their teaching as to whether
the divine image in man is a natural gift or something supernatural. Indeed, what renders some of their theories obscure lies
precisely in the effort of the writers to make practical experience
fit the neoplatonic framework instead of looking to Aristotle
and St. Thomas for a more graceful mode of philosophical
expression. Similarly, their preoccupation with the neoplatonic
"multiple" and the "one" gives rise to the idea that all the
faithful, without distinction, should be striving after nakedness
of spirit.

Of the immediate union substantially effected, Tauler writes:
"God acts in the soul by direct operation. He acts in that depth
where no image ever penetrates, which is only accessible to him;
this is what no creature is able to do";[73] and a little further on in

the same sermon he adds: "It is precisely because all images reach the soul from without, that *this mystery* of union is hidden from it, and this is a great advantage for it."[74] As we shall see later, the teaching of St. John of the Cross throws further light on this point.

It is difficult to state clearly what is meant by the expression "union without difference". Tauler seems to lose himself entirely in the "divine abyss" or "profound sea" into which he has been led by the gifts of wisdom and understanding; and Suso says that man in this union "forgets himself . . . no longer has knowledge of himself . . . disappears, loses himself in God, and becomes one mind with him, just as a little drop of water is drowned in a quantity of wine".[75] Again, he is insistent that this "powerful and annihilating return to nothingness causes, on the whole, *all difference to disappear*, not as regards being but as regards our way of understanding. . . . The soul always remains a creature; but when it is lost in nothingness, it does not know whether it is a creature or nothing; if it be united or not."[76]

Ruysbroeck, on the other hand, says that the love which brings about mystical union "is essentially one of joy", and he adds that "the distinction between itself and God is suppressed in the sense that the soul is made to enter into the same joy and beatitude as the divine essence".[77] That is quite possible, but one wonders what is meant by the statement: "Here beatitude is so simple and without plan that all essential contemplation fades away. . . ."[78] Such intensity of joy can certainly occur for varying periods of time, but as a permanent state it would have no practical purpose whatever. St. John of the Cross was later to say that "actual union" in all the powers of the soul "is not continuous, though the substantial union abides";[79] also St. Teresa was to insist that "*works* are the unmistakable sign which show these favours come from God".[80]

7  PRACTICAL  MYSTICISM  IN  THE  LOW  COUNTRIES
AND IN FRANCE

By the end of the fourteenth century, the popularity of the
German mystics had diminished steadily. Their doctrine was
not found sufficiently practicable, and exaggerations concerning
the voiding of self soon led to serious errors. A new system of
practical mysticism began to evolve, therefore, with the Brethren
of the Common Life and the Canons Regular of Windesheim as
its principal exponents.

The movement in Holland to which these reformers contributed, became known as the New Devotion, and its initiator
was a man of devout life called Gerard Groot (1340–84). The
Brethren of the Common Life, established as a confraternity in
1381, did not take vows but lived at a place called Deventer under
the authority of Gerard Groot and his disciple Florentius
Radewijns, dividing their time between spiritual exercises and
the copying of books. Gerard, who was in touch with Ruysbroeck, wanted to adopt the Rule of the Canons Regular of St.
Augustine but died without realizing this project. Later the
school of copyists at Deventer became associated with the
Canons Regular at Windesheim, but still remained distinct,
and by 1464 there were more than eighty such monasteries famed
for their copying work and sound moral influence. Later,
however, many went over to Protestantism and by the seventeenth century the rest had died out.

The spirituality of the Congregation of Windesheim was
very simple, and the writings of the times was mostly expressed
in the form of pious maxims. Gerlac Petersen, Henry de Mande,
and Thomas à Kempis are the names best known to us. Particular
stress was laid on the virtues of interior renunciation and
humility, patience, regular observance and mutual support.
*The Imitation of Christ* may or may not be the work of Thomas

à Kempis; at all events, his principal teaching about mystical love is contained in his *Cantica* and in his *Soliloquium animae*. It is known that he was acquainted with the teaching of Ruysbroeck, but he did not develop any new theories.

From the historical point of view, the New Devotion of Groot and Radewijns resulted mainly in the practice of spiritual exercises in a regulated form, and this was soon adopted by the Benedictines as well. The famous *Ejercitatorio de la vida espiritual* of Dom Garcia de Cisneros, a Spanish Benedictine and Abbot of Montserrat, was later to influence the founder of the Society of Jesus, St. Ignatius Loyola.

This reaction in the Low Countries from speculative mysticism was very mild, however, by comparison with the new movement in France as represented by Pierre d'Ailly and Jean Gerson, chancellors of the University of Paris. Pierre d'Ailly (1350–1420), the famous Cardinal Archbishop of Cambrai, was amongst the first to oppose the mystical exaggerations which, along with many other evils associated with the Great Schism, had taken root by the end of the fourteenth century. His own teaching, however, was not beyond criticism; and although he is known for his share in developing the cult of St. Joseph (as popularized by St. Bernard in the twelfth century), also for some of his writings on meditation and contemplation, the work of his disciple Jean Gerson is of much greater consequence.

Jean Gerson (1363-1429) is chiefly remarkable for his practical sense, a quality much needed by the end of the fourteenth century in France. He began by attacking agnostic mysticism, also those who exaggerated the negative idea of God to such an extent that nothing at all remained. He denied the assertion that the contemplative life is within the reach of all the faithful, and he insisted on the fundamental practices of asceticism, including meditation on the Passion and prudent direction, also on manual labour for those who aspired to the contemplative heights. Well did he know the immoral tendencies of many of those who claimed to be spiritual, also their obstinacy in clinging to doctrines of their own invention. Intellectual pride, in fact, nearly always terminates in moral delinquency, this being precipitated by diabolical interference.

Gerson's positive mystical teaching reveals his preference for the Victorines, also for the dogmatic method of St. Bonaventure, and Pourrat gives a clear account of the terminology used in his analysis.[81] Sensible reflexion, rational meditation, spiritual contemplation, these are his three steps towards ecstatic or beatifying love. Spiritual contemplation, in this context, is the same as that described by St. John of the Cross in the *Ascent of Mount Carmel*,[82] becoming known as "acquired contemplation" in the terminology of subsequent Carmelite writers in Spain. Gerson's mystical marriage requires a very high degree of abstraction for the intellect, and a no less intense detachment of the heart from every human satisfaction, so it is not surprising that he ruled out the contemplative vocation for the majority of the faithful, reserving his *Mountain of Contemplation* for the privileged few. He also wrote a treatise *On Meditation* and twelve treatises on the *Magnificat*. Pourrat, in a footnote, draws special attention to his wise counsel concerning the treatment of scruples.

## 8   OTHER EXAMPLES OF MYSTICISM DURING THE LATE MIDDLE AGES

In the Rhineland during the fifteenth century, reaction against mystical speculation came to be known as "Learned Ignorance", a name associated with Nicholas of Cusa and with several other noted theologians of the day.[83] Here the intellectual part of the soul became regarded as an obstacle to devotion, and it was suggested that the heights of contemplation might be attained through the simple exercise of spiritual will-power alone. Some went so far in this view that they merited censure from Jean Gerson. Others, like Nicholas of Cusa, were more moderate.

In England meanwhile, the two principal mystical writers had been: Walter Hilton (d. 1396), a Canon Regular of St. Augustine, best known for his *Scale of Perfection;* and Juliana of Norwich, the recluse famous for her book of *Revelations.*

In Italy, during the Great Schism, mysticism of the kind described by Gerson became very widespread. St. Lawrence Justinian (1380–1455), for example, exerted much influence by means of his ascetic treatises, sermons and spiritual letters. His general outlook was akin to that of Gerson, and his work for the Canons Regular of St. George is also well known. St. Frances of Rome (1384–1440) and St. Catherine of Genoa (1447–1510) were both outstanding for their spirit of charity and for the quality of their spiritual contemplation.

Carthusian life, during this same period, began to spread in Germany and became famous for its variety of practical mysticism. The first Carthusian monastery had been founded in 1084 at the Grande Chartreuse by St. Bruno (1032–1101), followed some eight years later by one at La Calabra in southern Italy where the founder died. From the beginning, a combination of the eremitical and coenobitical ideals had been envisaged, but the founder's traditions and customs were not codified till later. Ludolph the Carthusian (1300–70) became famous for his *Life of Christ;* then Dionysius the Carthusian published works to the extent of forty-five quarto volumes. Dionysius, who was known as "the ecstatic doctor" by reason of the time he spent in that uplifted state, was versed in every branch of philosophical and theological learning. His principal teaching on mystical theology is contained in a treatise entitled *On Contemplation,* and he is noteworthy for his distinction between active contemplation and that which requires a special vocation. His concept of the *patiens divina* of the Areopagite (the experimental *sensation* of the divine as compared with the simple *sense* of God's presence) resembles that of St. Thomas Aquinas and later St. John of the Cross.

Abbot Ludovicus Blosius (1506–66) is in the nature of a human connecting-link between the spirituality of the fourteenth century, the post-Reformation methods of the Jesuits, and the teaching of St. Teresa and St. John of the Cross. Ordained priest at the age of twenty-four, he was blessed as Abbot of Liessies in Belgium two days later, and devoted his whole life thereafter to the sanctification of himself, his monks, and all others with whom he had personal contact. His writings, including his *Instituto Spiritualis* (Book of Spiritual Instruction), reveal a mind exceptionally well balanced and well informed in every aspect of the interior life, affective as well as speculative, but with obvious personal experience of the mystical union described by Tauler and Ruysbroeck. On the other hand, he fully appreciated the work done in Louvain by the newly-founded Society of Jesus, and he used to send his monks there to be given the Exercises. The interior exercises, which he himself prescribes, resemble in many ways the "active night of sense" and the "active night of faith" as later described by St. John of the Cross, and his devotion to the Sacred Humanity is outstanding. The twelfth chapter of his *Instituto Spiritualis*, which describes in general terms something of the nature and delight of essential union with God, contains some of the most beautiful passages known to mystical theology. That all should aspire to this union, he defends on the grounds that "God will bestow upon us an eternal reward for our good desires, even though in this pilgrimage we may never attain to what we desire".[84] He admits, however, that "few indeed ever come to any experimental knowledge of the highest affection and simple intelligence, the highest point of the spirit and the hidden essence of the soul. Not only so, but it is almost impossible to persuade many men to believe that this hidden essence of the soul exists in us at all. . . . It is entirely simple . . . and the three higher powers are here united in one."[85] The *memoria* of William of St. Thierry, as we have seen, corresponds with what Blosius here calls "the simple eye" of the soul, "a pure, simple, uniform *thought*, raised above all reflexions of the intellect";[86] and this secret depth, wherein the *memoria* has been placed, is where Blosius says "the soul receives the hidden word" of God, the infused touch which effects "the happy embrace of mystical union".[87] In every way, the life and work of this "Doctor of the Presence of God" makes an interesting prelude to the Carmelite reforms in Spain, also to the complementary doctrines of St. Teresa and St. John of the Cross which we are about to examine.

[1]Quoted by the Holy Father when Abp. of Milan in his pastoral, *Man's Religious Sense*, trans. Darton, Longman & Todd, p. 14.

[2]*Proslogion*, cap. i; quoted by Pourrat, Vol. 2, pp. 14–15.

[3]*De fide Trinitatis*, cap. ii; quoted by Pourrat, p. 15.

[4]Cf. *Meditations* (P. L. CLVIII, 109–820).

[5]In tempore paschali, sermo iii, 3; quoted by Pourrat, p. 11.

[6]See Pourrat, Vol. 2, pp. 19–51.

[7]See In Cant. sermo xx, 6; also In Nat. Dom. sermo iii, 3 & 5.

[8]In Cant. sermo xlviii, 3; quoted by Pourrat, p. 43.

[9]In Nat. Dom. sermo i, 2; quoted by Pourrat, p. 43.

[10]In Cant. sermo lxxxiii, 3; quoted by Pourrat, p. 69.

[11]Cf. In Cant. sermo xxiii, 16.

[12]See Pourrat, Vol. 2, p. 70.

[13]Cf. In Cant. sermo xli, 3; see also Pourrat, p. 71.

[14]In Cant. sermo xxiii, 16; quoted by Pourrat, p. 70.

[15]See Pourrat, Vol. 2, pp. 51–63.

[16]Blosius, *Book of Spiritual Instruction*, p. 99.

[17]Op. cit., p. 95.

[18]See, for example, *De Trinitate XV*, xxi, 40, 41.

[19]Julius Tyciak, *Life in Christ*, trans. Wrighton, p. 36.

[20]In Cant. sermo xxxvi, I; quoted by Pourrat, p. 101.

[21]p. 780.

[22]p. 785.

[23]Epist. cxciii; quoted by Pourrat, pp. 102–3.

[24]See Pourrat, Vol. 2, pp. 109–17; cf. Dom Winzen, O.S.B., in *Symbols of Christ* (Longmans, Green & Co: Inner Life Series).

[25]Pourrat, Vol. 2, p. 121.

[26]See Pourrat, Vol. 2, pp. 120–9.

[27]*Benjamin Major*, lib. I, cap. vi; quoted by Pourrat, p. 123.

[28]See Part One, pp. 23–24.

[29]*Benjamin Major*, lib. V; quoted by Pourrat, pp. 127–8.

[30]Cf. *Benjamin Major*, lib. IV, cap. xxiii.

[31]See Pourrat, Vol. 2, pp. 135–51.

[32]See *S.T.*, I–II, q. 68.

[33]*S.T.*, II–II, q. 24, art. 8 (trans. Eng. Dominican Fathers).

[34]*S.T.*, II–II, q. 82, art. 1.

[35]*S.T.*, II–II, q. 44, art. 4.

[36]*S.T.*, II–II, q. 184, art. 4.

[37]See *S.T.*, II–II, q. 187, art. 3; q. 188, art. 5.

[38]See *S.T.*, I–II, qq. 55–67; also q. 71.

[39]Described by Pourrat, Vol. 2, p. 142.

[40]*S.T.*, II–II, q. 82, art. 3, ad. 1.

[41]See *S.T.*, II–II, q. 183.

[42]*S.T.*, I–II, q. 25, art. 2.

[43]See *S.T.*, I–II, q. 25, art. 3.

[44]*S.T.*, I–II, q. 59. art. 1.

[45]See Pourrat, Vol. 2, p. 148.

[46]Pourrat, Vol. 2, p. 149.

[47]See, for example, *De Veritate*, q. 18, art. 1.

[48]*S.T.*, II–II, q. 180, art. 4.

[49]*S.T.*, II–II, q. 175, art. 1.

[50]Ibid, art. 2.

[51]Ibid., art. 4.

[52]Ibid., art. 6.

[53]See *S.T.*, I–II, q. 65.

[54]See *S.T.*, II–II, q. 1, art. 3, ad.I.

[55]Leg. I, pp. 94–5; quoted by Pourrat, pp. 169–70.

[56]*Itinerarium mentis ad Deum.*

[57]*Acta Sancta*, cap. xi; see Pourrat, p. 193.

[58]Loc. cit.

[59]Pourrat, Vol. 2, p. 204.

[60]*Dialogue*, 2nd Answer, xlviii, xliv; quoted by Pourrat, p. 209.

[61]See Pourrat, Vol. 2, pp. 211–3.

[62]See Pourrat, Vol. 2, pp. 213–23.

[63]See Pourrat, Vol. 2, pp. 224–51 for a detailed description.

[64]*Institutions* of Tauler, Ch. xxvi; quoted by Pourrat, p. 229.

[65]Cf. Sermo I for 16th Sun. after Trinity, also Sermo I, Epiph.

[66]Sermo III for Pentecost, ii; quoted by Pourrat, p. 231.

[67]See Sermo for 9th Sun. after Trinity.

[68]*Book of Seven Cloisters*, Ch. 13; quoted by Pourrat, p. 233.

[69]See Ruysbroeck, *Mirror of Eternal Salvation*, xix, etc; cf. the fifteenth century treatise, *De Adhaerendo Deo*, cap. iv.

[70]*Institutions*, Ch. xxxv; quoted by Pourrat, p. 235.

[71]Sermo 2 for 20th Sun. after Trinity, ii; quoted by Pourrat, p. 237.

[72]Pourrat, Vol. 2, p. 238.

[73]Sermo for Sun. in Oct. of Christmas; quoted by Pourrat, p. 244.

[74]Loc. cit., p. 243.

[75]*Book of Truth*, iv; quoted by Pourrat, pp. 246–7.

[76]*Book of Truth*, v; quoted by Pourrat, p. 247.

[77]*Book of the Highest Truth;* quoted by Pourrat, p. 248.

[78]Loc. cit.

[79]*Spiritual Canticle*, xxvi; p. 141, Longman, Green & Co., 1864.

[80]*Interior Castle*, 7.4.10; p. 289, Baker Ed. 1921.

[81]See Pourrat, Vol. 2, pp. 278–83.

[82]Bk. 2, Chs. 13–14.

[83]See Vol. 2, p. 284, footnote.

[84]*Book of Spiritual Instruction*, pp. 81–2.

[85]p. 99.

[86]p. 84.

[87]p. 84.

## PART THREE

# THE SYNTHESES OF ST. TERESA AND ST. JOHN OF THE CROSS

## FOREWORD

BEFORE proceeding to the third part of our study, it may assist the reader to recall some of the more important theological points which have so far been noted. Pourrat has aptly described the Middle Ages as "a period in which spiritual doctrine was practised without having been fully synthetized".[1] In the intellectual sphere no less than in the moral sphere, nature and grace had developed side by side with such vigour that the difference between their operations was often hard to discern. Saints given to ecstasy and revelation enjoyed a popularity never surpassed either before or since, and they did not hesitate to utilize the esteem in which they were held for the purpose of urging interior reform for the Church. The women saints in particular—from St. Hildegarde in Germany and St. Bridget in Sweden to St. Catherine of Siena in Italy—seem to have regarded this task of reform as their own special mission; and we find this same thing happening in the late sixteenth century with the Italian ecstatics, namely St. Mary Magdalen de' Pazzi of the Florence Carmel and the Dominican nun St. Catherine de Ricci.

In this kind of spiritual atmosphere, always so highly charged with emotion, novel practices tended to spring up like weeds. Religious, it is true, were bound to respect the rule and constitutions of their order or congregation; but mystics in general had far more respect for their subjective inspirations than for ecclesiastical authority, let alone for the control of theological principles, and it was not until the time of Jean Gerson in France that effective progress was made in checking the vast overgrowth of counterfeit religious experience. The "angelic contemplation" of St. Thomas, on the other hand, was comprehended still less than it is today by the majority of interior souls; and even well-known writers or preachers like John Tauler tended to obscure the truth by confusing their spiritual teaching with the principles of Platonic idealism, by seeking to make their doctrine universal in its application, and by neglecting the practice of good works. Pourrat, at the beginning of his third volume on *Christian Spirituality*,[2] provides an excellent picture of the social and historical background occasioned by the Renaissance and the Protestant Reformation.

As regards the theological term "infused contemplation", the second part of this study should have made it abundantly clear that two distinct varieties of this phenomenon enjoy the approbation of the Church: the one *affective*, popular in character, and tending to be spectacular in its manifestations; the other *substantial*, demanding a total purification of the memory and understanding in addition to that of the will, and entirely hidden from the eyes of the world. As Abbot Blosius remarks in the eighth chapter of his *Book of Spiritual Instruction:* "Those things . . . that can be explained in words, are not very much; but those things which perfect men experience, when they are entirely absorbed in God and intimately united to him, are not able to be expressed in words or even comprehended in the mind."[3] The phenomenon known as "suspension of the faculties"—to lesser or greater degree—is present in affective contemplation only, and is mainly due to the intensity of the experience, especially when some nervous or physical weakness is also present; more rarely is it due to the direct act of God. "Ligature", on the other hand, is a *supernatural* negation of natural activity in the understanding and memory; and this, being effected through the gratuitous influence of infused faith and hope on these powers, gradually becomes an habitual characteristic of the soul to whom the angelic mode of contemplation is granted, especially during the times of formal mental prayer. The gifts of the Holy Ghost are the vehicles of actual grace in both types of experience, as much in the one as in the other; but a change in their mode of operation occurs, according as the light of faith gains habitual control of the intellectual faculty, and always this light of faith to the *natural* understanding or reason is a ray of darkness. As St. John of the Cross explains: "The wisdom of contemplation is the language of God addressed to the soul, purely spiritual, and the senses are not spiritual, so they do not perceive it, and so it remains a secret from them, they cannot understand it nor explain it."[4] Our study of the doctrine of St. Teresa and St. John of the Cross will throw further light on these distinctions.

## I   THE BACKGROUND TO CARMELITE TEACHING

Between the end of the sixth century and the middle of the seventh century, monastic rules for nuns and monks had been drawn up on simple Benedictine lines by successive archbishops of Seville. The Spanish temperament has always been a distinctive one, with strong mystical tendencies not necessarily orthodox, and this became a special danger during the sixteenth century owing to the illuminism so widespread at the time together with the false doctrines of the Protestant heresy. The situation was kept under control through the rigorous supervision of the Inquisition, but at serious cost to the development of spiritual theology. A great many potential books and treatises were left unwritten, and probably as many again were destroyed through fear or suspicion. As the particular genius of St. Teresa and St.

John of the Cross needs to be regarded from the historical standpoint, also against the background of contemporary writers, Pourrat's treatment of this subject[5] is to be recommended. For our present purpose, it will suffice to note only the more important doctrines and their human representatives.

Probably the greatest threat to Spanish orthodoxy was the philosophy of Averroes in the twelfth century,[6] which gave birth in the Arabian mind to a powerful ascetico-mystical theology as well. The Arabs are a deeply religious people, and the *terminus ad quem* proposed by Averroism is no less than union with God by means of speculative contemplation. Man, however, was thought to have no active intellect of his own, simply a passive one. Thus, in order to contemplate, he had to strive to identify his passive intellect with the divine Sun, the active intellectual principle common to all men, and in this consisted perfection. As regards the ascetical practices of the Arabians, these were described most fully by Algazel (d. 1111) and had been copied for the most part from those of the monks in the East. In the thirteenth century, Blessed Raymond Lull[7] did much towards checking the circulation of Arabian literature in Spain, also towards countering its pantheistic influence by means of Catholic spirituality. Then, in the fifteenth century, Cardinal Ximenes de Cisneros (also a Franciscan, and a relation of the famous Abbot of Monserrat) continued this important work of neutralizing the hold on Christian minds of Arabian learning. This, however, did not suffice to check the immorality and quietistic practices of the Albigenses and the Beghards whose influence became particularly strong towards the end of the Middle Ages.

The influence of the sect known as the Alumbrados began to make itself felt in Andalusia about the year 1509. At that point in history, its doctrine was still vague but it aimed at the encouragement of quietistic practices generally, also at stirring up excessive emotionalism. Many were deceived by the phenomena produced, and even the inquisitors had the utmost difficulty in checking this diabolical activity. Edicts were issued in 1568, 1574 and 1623; and on this third occasion, the doctrines of the false mystics were condemned under the heading of thirty-five separate propositions. Many of these propositions were later revived by Michael Molinos.

The aim of the Franciscan writers during the first half of the sixteenth century was to check illuminism by increasing the number of books available in the vernacular. Cardinal Ximenes had been the great pioneer of this work, but at the time of his death in 1517 his success was still limited to providing Spain with translations of foreign spiritual works.

At Seville in 1521, Alonso of Madrid published an ascetic treatise entitled *The Art of Serving God*, which later merited the commendation of St. Teresa. The first part is concerned with the general principles of interior perfection, the second part with basic ascetical practices, the third part with divine love but only to a restricted degree.

At Toledo in 1527, Francisco of Ossuna published a treatise on the prayer of recollection entitled *The Third Primer of Spirituality*, which had a great influence on St. Teresa and supplied her with a basic pattern when writing her own *Life*. Thus Francisco taught that there are four degrees in this prayer: "the recollection which gently quiets the powers of the soul; that in which the intelligence is still working; a more perfect kind in which the soul becomes enclosed within itself . . . for the enjoyment of God; and ecstatic recollection".[8] Such, in fact, are the degrees of affective contemplation as already noted in this study.

At Seville in 1535, Bernardino of Laredo[9] published a similar treatise on the prayer of affective quiet and union, and this was used by St. Teresa about the year 1556 during a period of extreme aridity.

At Lisbon, between the years 1556 and 1560, St. Peter of Alcantara published a treatise on *Prayer and Meditation*, the intended fruit of which was to be measured in terms of devotion to duty. This appears to be a summary of a similar work by Luis of Granada, together with some account of the author's own experience. The importance of meditation as a means to contemplation is stressed, but also the fact that the soul must cease from this exercise once the quiet of contemplation has been tasted. So long as the soul is capable of affective acts, all discursive effort on the part of the understanding is to be excluded. Like St. Teresa, however, St. Peter of Alcantara was convinced that it was wrong to try to anticipate grace in this respect or to try to paralyse the activity of the mind before God himself has led the soul into quietude.

Luis of Granada (1505–88) was one of the most powerful Dominicans in the spiritual crusade against the Alumbrados and the Protestants. His method of prayer for Christians living in the world was similar to that of the Jesuit founder, St. Ignatius Loyola, and he avoided mystical subjects as far as possible on account of the Inquisition. None the less, he looked upon the prayer of recollection and quietude as the goal of meditation, and he enlarged on this subject in his *Libro de la Oracion*. Pedro Ibanez (d. 1565) was the first of three Dominican confessors to direct St. Teresa in the ways of extraordinary prayer, and the first draft of her *Life* (drawn up in 1562 and now lost) was written in obedience to him. About the year 1563 or 1564, he wrote a report giving his approval to the interior ways of the saint. Dominico Banez (1528–1604) also testified to the Inquisition concerning the integrity of St. Teresa, but he was more cautious about circulating the book of her *Life*. He was confessor at St. Joseph's, Avila, between the critical years 1562 and 1568, and was instrumental in saving the foundation from ruin.

Blessed John of Avila, a secular priest born in 1500 and famed for his apostolic work in Andalusia, was even less partial than Banez to visions and revelations, and he advised St. Teresa to be as detached as possible from all such experiences. He himself had great devotion to the Sacred Humanity and is best known for his mystical commentary entitled *Audi, filia, et vide.*

At Toledo in 1551, the first index of the Inquisition was published by Fernando de Valdes, Archbishop of Seville. Heterodox versions of the Bible were excluded, including those of the Jews and the Lutherans, and no version might be read in the vernacular. These measures, however, had small effect on the heresies of the day, with the result that every spiritual treatise became suspect. As time went on, no one dared to speak or write freely, and when St. Teresa was informed in 1575 that the book of her *Life* had been denounced to the Holy Office, she greatly feared that this might destroy the whole work of her Reform. This threat was averted, however, thanks to Dominico Banez and his favourable report.

Balthazar Alvarez (1533–80) became director to St. Teresa when he was only twenty-five, three years after he had joined the Society of Jesus. He tried to make her practise discursive prayer exclusively and exercised her virtues in every possible way. Finally, however, he came to believe in her, and on account of this belief he himself had to suffer. In the year 1567, he too began to experience the interior effects of affective quiet and union.

Amongst the Augustinian writers, Luis de Leon (1527–91) was one of the greatest men of letters in Spain during the second half of the sixteenth century. Some years after his imprisonment at the hands of the inquisitors, he wrote a masterpiece entitled *The Names of Christ*, and so great was the knowledge and authority attributed to him that he was later asked to take charge of the publication of St. Teresa's writings. He was also a famous poet.

Thomas d'Andrada (1530–82) portrayed the sufferings of Jesus rather than his glories, and his method of meditation was akin to that of Luis of Granada. For him, the spiritual life consisted in two things: mortification and the love of God. If mortification did not lead to the love of God, then it was to be held suspect.

These biographical notes, though brief, throw useful light on the subject-matter of the next two sections, especially in regard to the teaching of St. Teresa whose personal convictions do not become fully apparent prior to her writing of the *Interior Castle*. She first met St. John of the Cross in September 1567, five years before attaining to the seventh mansion, and none can doubt the extent of his influence in freeing her from the deep interior anguish to which she was subject at the time. As doctor of the theological virtues in their relation to contemplation, his teaching is in many ways unique.


2   THE DOCTRINE OF ST. TERESA IN RELATION TO
ST. JOHN OF THE CROSS

In the person of St. Teresa of Avila (1515–82), we are presented with the first living synthesis of mystical experience in all its most important forms. Previously we have met with countless examples of heroic virtue, also of mystical experience in its affective, speculative and extraordinary manifestations; also we have observed something of the influence over society which these special friends of God were empowered to exert. With St. Teresa, however, we find all these things being manifested, to lesser or greater degree, in the course of her own life; and, most outstanding of all, is her Christ-centred spirit of virtue, her self-devotion to Jesus as emperor of her entire being. From the lives of such men as Dionysius the Carthusian and Abbot Blosius, one could begin to guess that such a synthesis might be possible within a single soul; but certainly the Church has never known the like of St. Teresa's powers of first-hand description in regard to these varied experiences. As she herself used to say, the art of explaining a grace and of making it sound intelligible to others is something quite distinct from merely receiving the grace and appreciating it for oneself alone. To generalize is not her way at all. She observes the facts as closely as possible, then leaves the theologians to theorize about them. This psychological method has many advantages, but it can also prove bewildering; so, in the interest of clarity and precision, brief references to the corresponding doctrine of St. John of the Cross will also be made in the course of this section.

*The Interior Castle*, which was written in 1577, is by far the most mature of St. Teresa's works; and it is interesting to notice that she always refers to its mansions in terms of light, above all the seventh mansion which is the secret dwelling-place of the King of Glory. This brightness, it is true, is darkness to the natural understanding, but not so to the eyes of faith. The castle then, as is well known, represents the Christian soul; and the entrance-gate is *prayer*, because this alone—according as the King issues the invitation—enables the soul to recollect itself and to enter within. Up to the age of sixteen, St. Teresa was largely taken up with worldly frivolities and the reading of chivalrous romances; but through illness she came to recognize how little the world has to offer, and in the course of her twenty-second year she finally resolved to abandon the occasions of sin by entering the Carmelite convent in Avila. In the convent she was protected against serious temptation, but even so she found herself subject to periods of interior slackness. Her natural popularity and gift of friendship made her reluctant to withdraw from the diversions of the parlour, and for nearly twenty years our Lord permitted her to experience the depths of her natural weakness. The precise date is uncertain, but the transverberation of her heart is said to have occured between the years 1559 and 1562. Previous to that, she had experienced an imaginative vision of hell, together with other supernatural elevations of an interior kind. Finally in 1572, ten years before her death, she attained to the transforming union of the seventh mansion, and was thus enabled to record—with unparalleled accuracy—the nature and practical effects of spiritual marriage when granted substantially.

The Teresian divisions of prayer have given rise to endless discussions, especially as to where the mystical dividing-line should be placed. The plan of her *Life*, as we have seen, clearly originates in the theories of affective contemplation which she had learned from the Franciscan writers, and if we wish to discover what she really had in mind when distinguishing four degrees of extraordinary or mystical prayer, we have only to refer back to the *Third Primer of Spirituality*. Thus Francisco's first degree of recollection is the equivalent of St. Teresa's prayer of Infused Recollection; his second degree corresponds with St. Teresa's prayer of Quiet as described in the fifteenth chapter of her *Life;* his third degree corresponds with St. Teresa's prayer of Union as described in the sixteenth chapter of her *Life;* and his fourth degree is the same as St. Teresa's prayer of Ecstatic Union as described in the eighteenth to twenty-first chapters of her *Life*. We must notice, however, that St. Teresa in the seventeenth chapter of her *Life* refers to three distinct varieties of union, two of which are not included in the Franciscan scheme, namely the experience of involuntary distraction in prayer, and the state of prayer wherein Mary and Martha have come to terms. This will be referred to again. For the present, the important point to note is that the terms *quiet* and *union* are always modified by the particular context in which St. Teresa uses them. The task of co-relating the *Life* and the *Interior Castle* and the *Way of Perfection* (this last being in the nature of a practical sequel to the *Life*) is by no means easy, and the tendency of modern theologians is to see how the teaching of St. Teresa will fit in with their own preconceived schemes. Such a method does not do justice to her own original approach, still less to her actual experience which was built up gradually at the expense of great interior suffering, so we cannot do better than examine each stage of St. Teresa's development according as it is laid down for us.

St. Teresa in the eleventh chapter of her *Life* likens the spiritual beginner to a person trying to make a garden in un-cultivated soil, a garden wherein our Lord will ultimately delight to take his rest. In this, His Majesty assists her, pulling up the weeds and planting seedlings of virtue in their place; but the initial task of *watering* these plants is still her own responsibility, and she must exercise all her ingenuity to ensure their growth. The first and most arduous method of irrigation (the equivalent of discursive prayer) is to draw the water from a well. Secondly, as an elaboration of the first method, a windlass (the equivalent of ordinary affective prayer) may be operated in conjunction with a system of buckets and water-wheel already set up. The proximity of a stream or brook is even more advantageous; and best of all, of course, is the heavy rain which the Lord in his goodness may sometimes give for the saturation of the land. This comparison, then, gives St. Teresa her point of departure for talking about four degrees of prayer; but we must not get confused and think that these are the same as the four methods of watering referred to above. The former, as we have seen, refer to the four degrees of affective contemplation, whereas the latter describe the means whereby the soul may hope to attain to interior fruition.

Prayer of the first water, then, requires great effort and generous perseverance, for it comprises all the active means whereby the soul may hope to dispose itself for the first degree of supernatural recollection (including the basic erection of the water-wheel system). A good deal of overlapping occurs in St. Teresa's descriptions, but this is the practical meaning of what she teaches. In the fourth to thirteenth chapters of her *Life*, she makes various useful recommendations concerning the active methods of prayer, but in no place does she insist that beginners should be restricted to any one method. Many souls, it is true, find support during these early stages in a book of meditations systematically arranged, but many more resemble St. Teresa in that they lack the ability to apply their spiritual faculties in the manner prescribed. In her own case, we find that prayerful reading was the greatest help, also the cultivation of intimate friendship with Jesus and Mary. Simple thoughts about the Passion, the sight of a devotional picture or statue, the beauties of nature, all these things helped to raise her mind and heart from the wretchedness of self. Vocal prayers, repeated slowly and attentively, likewise helped her to calm her imagination as a means of recollection.[10]

St. John of the Cross, we must note, does not profess to write on this subject but neither does he belittle its importance. In the third stanza of the *Living Flame*, for example, he says of this state of beginners: "We must keep in mind that it is one of meditation and of acts of reflexion. It is necessary to furnish the soul in this state with matter for meditation, that it may make reflexions and those interior acts, and avail itself of the sensible spiritual heat and fervour, for this is necessary in order to accustom the senses and desires to good things, so that by satisfying them by the sweetness thereof they may be detached from the world."[11] The ascetical doctrine of St. John of the Cross will be discussed in the next section of this study.

The Teresian prayer of Recollection belongs to the first water (when active), to the second water (when associated with the prayer of Quiet as described in the fourth mansion of the *Interior Castle*). Thus St. Teresa, in the fourteenth chapter of her *Life*, says that this state wherein the soul begins to recollect itself in an active manner, closely approaches that supernatural experience to which none can attain by their own efforts; but in this particular context she calls it the prayer of Quiet, whereas this same term has entirely different connotations both in the thirty-first chapter of the *Way of Perfection* and in the fourth mansion of the *Interior Castle*. It is important to notice this. St. Teresa's considerations based on the words "who art in heaven"[12] are amongst the most beautiful of all her writings. The kingdom of God is within us; that is the vital point, and there is nothing but ignorance and false humility in the attitude of those who deny this fact or act as if it were of no importance to the soul in a state of grace. Each individual, it is true, has to find the method of approach to our Lord best suited to his or her own psychology —for example, the way of a sister, a brother, a spouse, a trusting child—but common to all is the spirit of recollection engendered when the soul begins to recognize that no lasting happiness is to be found apart from His Majesty. Sufferings, too, had a very important part to play in developing St. Teresa's interior life; and after some three years of painful nervous illness beginning about 1538, she found herself being raised in a transitory manner to the prayer of affective Quiet and Union.

According to St. John of the Cross, there are three signs of contemplation and interior recollection in the soul, but these have to be found together. First, there is the absence of pleasure in transitory things; secondly, there is the positive desire to strive after greater perfection in solitude and silence; thirdly, there is genuine difficulty in practising discursive prayer. This degree of recollection corresponds with the third mansion of St. Teresa, but it is important to notice that St. John of the Cross arrives at it by an intellectual road. The term "active recollection" may be used quite safely in describing both experiences, but the indiscriminate use of the terms "prayer of simplicity", "active contemplation", "acquired contemplation" and "prayer of simple regard" can be seriously misleading.

Infused Recollection, as stated at the beginning of the last paragraph, belongs more properly to the Quiet of the fourth mansion, but St. Teresa herself distinguishes the one from the other both in her *Interior Castle* and in her *Fifth Spiritual Relation* as written from Seville in 1576. Describing this prayer, St. Teresa refers first to our Lord as a great king dwelling within the mansion of the soul, then as a shepherd seeking to round up the straying members of his flock. In both cases, it is our Lord himself who takes the initiative in drawing souls away from their worldly distractions and bringing them back to the fortified castle of which he is the master. St. Teresa then goes on to enumerate the reasons why she is convinced that the soul should not try to induce this passive recollection through deliberate silencing of the understanding,[13] and in the twenty-second chapter of her *Life* she enlarges on this subject. Here she insists particularly on the value of devotion to the Sacred Humanity, both as the way leading to the highest contemplation and as our refuge in times of trial or inward affliction.

In the teaching of St. John of the Cross, the three signs of infused recollection (the contemplation of progressives) are fully described in the thirteenth and fourteenth chapters of the *Ascent of Mount Carmel*, Book 2, and these signify before all else *progression in prayer*, progression towards the hidden Beloved. In the same way, St. John of the Cross has stated that "if a soul has more patience under suffering, a greater endurance in the absence of sweetness, that is a sign of greater progress in virtue".[14]

The prayer of Quiet ("divine tastes") is an intensified form of infused recollection and probably represents most closely what St. Teresa meant by prayer of the second water, though we have to make allowances for the ambiguity of her terminology at an earlier stage. In the sixth chapter of her *Life*, she acknowledges the influence of this prayer on her affective powers; and in the fourth mansion of her *Interior Castle*, after describing the dilation of soul due to this same prayer, she contrasts its natural misery with the wonders of grace which God may now work in it. "In short, its virtues are increased and it will not cease to advance in perfection unless it turns back and offends God," notably through spiritual pride, indiscretion and disobedience; but if it does presume to offend God in this way, it stands to lose everything "however high the state it may have reached".[15] That is why St. Teresa, in the last part of this chapter, is so careful to note the dangers of excessive absorption.[16] Such graces of infused consolation are given to the soul for no other reason than to lead it into the narrow path of pure faith and hope; therefore they must be used with humility, gratitude and simple detachment.

St. John of the Cross draws special attention to this prayer at the beginning of his *Obscure Night*, Book I, where he likens the divine caresses to those of a tender mother suckling her baby. Souls thus favoured are tempted to lose all restraint in yielding themselves to the intoxication of the moment, forgetting how weak and imperfect they really are, and little suspecting how lost they will feel when the infused consolations are withdrawn. Sooner would they die than be weaned from this state of contemplative babyhood.

The sequel to this kind of prayer of Quiet (which may include some experience of affective union as well) varies according to the dispositions of the soul. After St. Teresa's initial experience of it (as recorded in the sixth chapter of her *Life*) her desire for solitude increased, also her love for reading good books, and through the intercession of St. Joseph she obtained a cure for her physical maladies; but the return of her health did not help her to advance in the life of prayer. Prayer indeed became so difficult that she gave it up, and then she was afraid to try to resume it. God seemed to be calling her by means of inward attraction, yet her senses were still tied by the spirit of the world, and she did not yet know how to reconcile the conflicting claims on her time and energy. It was fortunate for our own instruction, but certainly not for her peace of mind at that stage, that there was no St. John of the Cross available to set her feet securely on the path leading to substantial contemplation in union with His Majesty. Few souls make headway in the obscure night without the grace of clear-cut assurance from one who knows the way; instead, they walk backwards or round in circles inevitably hoping to recover the sort of contemplation perceptible to the ordinary interior senses, the contemplation which will dilate the heart and bring relief to the body. It must be repeated, then, that the purpose of the graces of infused consolation is to lead the soul into the way of pure faith and hope, achieving this through the blinding effect of the infused light upon the natural understanding. Further, no matter how restless and bewildered the understanding may feel in this new state of aridity, the will must never withdraw from its determination to remain united to God alone.

Such a withdrawal might seem to solve the problem for the time being, but it would merely pave the way for still greater bewilderment and darkness of soul later on. St. Teresa therefore urges the practice of humility and gratitude, telling the soul to refer all its troubles to His Majesty and to be perfectly confident of his power and willingness to show it what to do. Having known herself what it was like to lack this conviction, she could in the end write all the more feelingly about it.

St. John of the Cross likens this phase of development to that of an infant in the process of being weaned, and he points out that adequate time for growth must be taken into consideration. Interior perfection is a relative term and must necessarily depend on the degree of supernatural virtue present in the soul.

Prayer of the third water, which is sometimes called "sleep of the powers", has many points in common with that of the second water; but whereas the soul in the prayer of Quiet experienced such extreme reluctance to withdraw from its contemplative absorption, here it discovers that the duties of its state are a help rather than a hindrance to deeper union with the Master. In other words, the interior orientation of the soul to God is now so strong that it has gained the ascendancy over everything that is less than God, and this gives rise to a spirit of holy indifference as to how it should be occupied. St. Teresa, in her *Way of Perfection*, describes this state as "a great favour to these souls, for the active and contemplative life are here combined";[17] and in her *Fifth Spiritual Relation* (written in 1576), she again stresses these same points. Such, then, is *the beginning* of the objective or substantial union in the soul, as distinct from the subjective union which is overwhelmingly affective in character.

St. John of the Cross observes that the soul whom God desires to lead forward, from meditation to contemplation, becomes as it were "wounded by love", and he enlarges on this subject in the first eleven stanzas of his *Spiritual Canticle*. The soul in this state does not cease of its own volition to practise discursive prayer, but finds that the power so to act has been withdrawn. This awareness of having been "wounded" corresponds with St. Teresa's teaching about prayer of the third water.

The affective prayer of Union marks the beginning of the prayer of the fourth water as described by St. Teresa in her *Life*, and although it is not of common experience, neither is it so rare as some would suppose. This is not the mystical union essential to St. Teresa's fifth mansion, but a still more lofty intensification of the affective experience which characterizes the fourth mansion, one which even borders on ecstasy and rapture. Here, as St. Teresa stresses in the eighteenth chapter of her *Life*, contact with God is maintained by *the will*, with the result that it is not long before the experience is interrupted. One is reminded in fact of a person trying to prolong a consoling dream, because the will—on discovering that the mind has woken up and may presently start thinking of other things—induces it to revert to slumber. This type of experience, although it occurs when least expected, is often the outcome of a long period of mental prayer, and the subsequent reaction on those who are physically weak is often one of nervous exhaustion. Other effects of this prayer include the mystical gift of tears, the urge to make heroic resolutions or promises, and also a new awareness of the wretchedness of the soul when separated from God. Nevertheless there is still scope for error, and St. Teresa at the end of the nineteenth chapter of her *Life* makes no secret of the way in which she herself was deceived by the devil. The tragedy is that so many interior souls are either ignorant of this warning or else will not pay heed to it, believing instead that their own experiences are in some way unique.

St. John of the Cross, in the first book of the *Obscure Night*, leaves no stone unturned to convince souls of the superior value of ordering their lives in Christ by means of pure faith and hope. "That light guided me," he says in the fourth stanza of the poem, "more surely than the noonday sun to the place where he was waiting for me."[18] These secret meetings between lover and Beloved belong to the essence of mystical contemplation.

The prayer of mystical Union, as found in the fifth mansion, should always be distinguished from *the degree of virtue* peculiar to that mansion. The latter is within the reach of every soul in a state of grace; the former is wholly gratuitous. This distinction, concerned as it is with the *means* of identification between the soul and Christ, is more apparent in the original Spanish than in any of the translations of St. Teresa's works, and it should be noted carefully. On the one hand, then, His Majesty in the prayer of mystical union manifests himself to the soul in its secret depth without in any way using the door of the senses. The experience, by reason of its sublimity, is hidden from the devil and defeats all human expression; but, as St. Teresa says, it is impossible for the soul to doubt "that it dwelt in him and that he was within it".[19] Only if we try to produce these touches of union by our own volition, do we expose ourselves to diabolical interference, and even then we cannot produce the deep peace and joy which characterize the work of God. "In order to declare his wondrous works more clearly," St. Teresa says, "he will leave us no share in them except complete conformity of our wills to his and abandonment of all things."[20] What does St. Teresa mean by this conformity and abandonment? She means that we must take as our example a busy little silk-worm building the cocoon wherein it will die, and from which it will then emerge to begin life again as a graceful little butterfly. Equivalent to the mulberry leaves, for the human soul, are all the means of actual and sacramental grace which come to it daily through Christ and his Church, but the degree of its vigour or spirit of faith depends even more particularly on its perseverance in prayer and meditation. Assisted by His Majesty, we shall die to ourselves in the cocoon of our own construction as surely as if the work had been done for us. Either way, the success of the building depends on the merits of our Lord's Passion and death; also, whatever reward may be withheld from us here on earth, it will not be withheld from us in heaven. The fifth mansion, then, reveals a state of mystical union characterized by extraordinary beauty and delicacy. In a striking comparison, St. Teresa likens it to one of pre-betrothal between two persons contemplating holy matrimony,[21] and she shows with what tact the divine Spouse sets about winning the confidence of his little bride. Further, she shows how the devil may still try to hinder the full betrothal and marriage, even although he is powerless to interfere with the substantial communications now taking place. From the devil's point of view, it is worth his while to marshal all the powers in hell if he may thereby prevent a soul from attaining to spiritual marriage; and on God's side too, it is as well that the soul be tested by fire before he grants her still deeper privileges.

St. John of the Cross, in the fourth stanza of the *Living Flame*, states that the "sweet embracing" of mystical union "takes place in the inmost substance and powers of the soul".[22] Then he goes on to explain the different degrees of indwelling which may be effected within the soul, and he stresses the fact that neither the devil nor the understanding of any man can attain to the secret depth wherein is granted this touch of union.

This is not so, however, in the forms of supernatural communication which the soul may experience *before entering*
the obscure night, because here there tends to be interference
from the senses. As St. John of the Cross puts it: "The senses
are not perfectly annihilated before the union is complete, and
they manifest their power in some degree because they are not
yet wholly subject to the spirit. But in this awakening of the
Bridegroom in the perfect soul, all is perfect because he effects
it all himself."[23]

St. Teresa, in the twentieth chapter of her *Life*, first writes
about the *affective* phenomena peculiar to ecstatic union, then
about the essential experience. For many years, she herself was
an ecstatic of an exceptionally high order; yet her many and varied
experiences in this field were permitted for the benefit or instruction of others rather than for herself, and she would have been
spared much suffering (both at the hands of her confessors
and from diabolical interference) if she had been trained from the
beginning by a director like St. John of the Cross. A soul given
to the experience of extraordinary phenomena has always to pay
for them in the hard coin of humiliation, misunderstanding and
fear of delusions. Sometimes too, on account of the weakness of
the body, ecstasy is permitted by way of relief to the soul during
the critical period of passive purification which precedes its entry
into the kingdom of the seventh mansion. Rapture, elevation,
flight of the spirit, transport and ecstasy, all denote the same
thing in Teresian language. Rapture, however, includes the
following particular characteristics: lightness of body, distur-
bances of consciousness, intermittent suspension of the faculties,
absence of strength, subsequent improvement of health, and
perfect conformity with God's designs for the soul. Suffering of
an extraordinary nature, such as the soul in this state may ex-

perience, are given by St. Teresa in the first chapter of the fifth mansion of her *Interior Castle*.

St. John of the Cross, at the beginning of the second book of his *Obscure Night*, attributes the accidental features of these phenomena to bodily or sensual weakness, and in his *Spiritual Canticle* he refers readers to the writings of "the blessed Teresa of Jesus".[24]

After describing the effects of rapture, St. Teresa refers in the twentieth chapter of her *Life* to another type of interior distress, and she makes it clear that this experience occurred more recently than the other visions and revelations with which she had been favoured. This, in fact, is the essential detachment or nakedness of spirit which characterizes the period of transition between spiritual betrothal (sixth mansion) and spiritual marriage (seventh mansion); and although in St. Teresa's case rapture seems to have been the means of producing it, there are other ways by which the divine action can penetrate the innermost recesses of the soul, causing the faculties to be dislocated by suffering, just as they are through the intensity of joy in union and rapture. During this time of trial, the soul has eyes for none but our Lord and avails herself of every opportunity to be alone, without however neglecting the duties of her state. Ordinarily her sufferings will be associated with a deep sense of personal failure, with difficulties in prayer, and with general forgetfulness. Misunderstandings and criticisms from others may be multiplied, and confession may become a trial since the faults committed by a soul in this state in no way correspond with its overwhelming feeling of having been cast off by God. Relief is sought but without any lasting effect. Indeed, St. Teresa tells us, "there is no other remedy in such a tempest except to wait for the mercy of God". The moment he dispels these sorrows, "every cloud of trouble disappears and the mind is left full of light and far happier than before".[25] Thus does His Majesty convince the soul of its inability to achieve any victory or other lasting good without the divine assistance.

St. John of the Cross, in his remarks preceding the thirteenth stanza of the *Spiritual Canticle*, puts it this way: "The comfort and consolations of God are, by his infinite goodness, proportional to the darkness and emptiness of the soul"; therefore "he sends into the soul, in the midst of its weariness, certain divine rays of himself . . . to stir it up from its very depths and to change its whole natural condition".[26]

The actual call to spiritual marriage involves several interior effects which St. Teresa describes in the second chapter of the sixth mansion: first, the intensification of pain and desire and strange distress; secondly, the experience of a certain interior fragrance betokening the nearness of His Majesty; thirdly, the experience of locutions, especially those involving the spiritual sense of hearing; fourthly, a type of rapture wherein the interior senses are not lost but are caught up in a certain wordless experience of the liberating power of the divine compassion.

St. John of the Cross indicates that varying lengths of time may be required before the final purifications and positive preparations on the part of God are completed, since he works here in accordance with the dispositions of the soul. It must be noted, however, that "the desire for God" is in itself "a disposition for union with him".[27]

St. Teresa's teaching about the seventh mansion, together with the spiritual marriage which takes place therein, is exceptionally lucid. At an earlier stage, it is true, she had been granted a vision wherein she was able to penetrate the depths of her soul, seeing our Lord there as if through transparent glass; but that was no more than a delicate foreshadowing of the deeper grace yet to come. Here, she tells us, "God appears in the soul's centre, not by an imaginary but by an intellectual vision far more mystic than those seen before . . . (and) in a far more subtle way than by . . . spiritual delight. As far as can be understood, the soul, I mean the spirit of this soul, is made one with God." By means of this union he binds himself to her "as firmly as two human beings are joined in wedlock and will never separate himself from her".[28] St. Teresa then emphasizes this new characteristic of indissolubility by contrasting it with the earlier graces of union and of spiritual betrothal. From now on, she says, "the soul *always remains* in its centre with its God".[29] St. Teresa does not claim impeccability for the soul, even although it is now so highly favoured and protected against serious temptation. At times, too, she appears to contradict her claim always to be at peace, but the key to this paradox is to be found in the distinction which she makes between *the powers* and *the substance* of the powers. Her teaching on this point is illustrated admirably in the last paragraph of the second chapter of her seventh mansion.

As regards the practical effects of spiritual marriage, in the Teresian sense of the term, the first and greatest is the self-forgetfulness born of the soul's determination to seek nothing but the honour of God. The second effect concerns its desire to suffer in the interests of Jesus Crucified, peacefully however, and with great interior joy. The third effect is one of detachment from all that does not pertain directly to God and his manifest plans; further, the soul has no fear "that this sublime favour can be counterfeited by the devil", possessing rather "a settled conviction that it is of divine origin".[30] Fourthly, few—if any—raptures are now experienced, the reason being that the cardinal virtues now maintain a new state of balance in the soul, offsetting its natural weakness or tendency to go to extremes of devotion.

St. John of the Cross, in the *Spiritual Canticle*, describes this new
   stability of soul by saying: "The dove-soul returns to the ark
   of God, not only white and pure as it went forth when he
   created it, but with the olive branch of reward and peace
   obtained by the conquest of itself."[31]

No saint has insisted more on the importance of fruition in
regard to the interior exercises of the soul than did St. Teresa.
"Oh, my sisters!" she exclaims, "how forgetful of her ease, how
unmindful of honours, and how far from seeking man's esteem
should she be whose soul God thus chooses for his special
dwellingplace! For if her mind is fixed on him, as it ought to be,
she must needs forget herself: all her thoughts are bent on how
to please him better and when and how she can show the love
she bears him."[32] The essential points concerning the ascetical
doctrine of St. Teresa will be included in the next section. In a
word, these may be described as the art of giving pleasure to the
Beloved, of returning to him the love which he has bestowed
upon us in the name of the most holy Trinity, Amen.

3   THE DOCTRINE OF ST. JOHN OF THE CROSS IN
             RELATION TO ST. TERESA

The impression left on the mind by Teresian spirituality is
strongly positive. Aridities and other trials are noted from a
psychological point of view, but it is only in the sixth mansion
of the *Interior Castle* that the reader is introduced fully to that
"state" of natural failure or nothingness which characterizes the
soul on the narrow path to substantial union and personal
oneness with its Creator. With St. John of the Cross, on the
other hand, the approach to the interior life is much more
scientific, and this makes the whole question of contemplation

seem correspondingly abstract. Beginners, and even those with some practical experience of the interior ways, usually find it difficult to decide what the Mystical Doctor is really talking about, and often his writings are criticized because they fail to coincide with someone else's ideas. The problems which arise, however, are mostly concerned with the ascetical conduct of the soul on its journey to God in Christ Jesus; so, in this present section, our purpose is to explore exactly the same interior paths as before, only this time from the point of view of the virtues to be practised therein. As St. Teresa insists in the last chapter of her *Interior Castle:* "Your foundation must not consist of prayer and contemplation alone: unless you acquire the virtues and practise them, you will always be dwarfs."[33]

In the first book of the *Ascent of Mount Carmel*, where he is treating of the conduct of beginners, St. John of the Cross says that "the estate of divine union consists in the total transformation of the will into the will of God, in such a way that every movement of the will shall be always the movement of the will of God only".[34] Such is the basic ideal proposed to theological charity and the infused moral virtues, an ideal to which every Christian in the state of grace can and should aspire; but in the third book of the *Ascent of Mount Carmel*, where St. John of the Cross is addressing a restricted number of souls of the type proficient already in charity and the contemplation of love, his object is to show that our interior transformation is not complete until the Spirit of God has taken full possession of the understanding and memory as well. In order therefore to predispose themselves for this perfection, souls to whom this special vocation has been given must continue to exercise their faculties in pure faith and hope, abandoning their former habit of relying on the evidence of the senses, and avoiding especially all extraordinary phenomena in relation to their prayer. Only thus will they dispose themselves to make further progress. Not all, however, are called to serve God in the same way, neither is the state of conformity to God's will the condition of contemplative graces being given to the soul. If God sees fit to withhold these graces, perfection then consists in accepting this dispensation of his providence, not in trying to induce consoling experiences. Those who presume to enter upon the obscure night of understanding and memory without the necessary interior stability and gratuitous vocation from God, end by losing everything, even as St. Teresa warns her readers in the twenty-second chapter of her *Life*. If the doctrine of St. John of the Cross is to be evaluated fully, these points must be recognized and appreciated from the outset.

In the first book of the *Ascent*, also in chapters 16–45 of the third book, St. John of the Cross describes in detail the active steps that the soul may take towards preparing itself for the first graces of contemplation. This active way of self-renunciation, which should always accompany the Teresian prayer of the first water, has the particular aim of strengthening the natural will-power of the soul at a time when the understanding is still darkened by sin and self-indulgence, and the practical judgement tends to be upset by the heat of passion. The means which it proposes are summarized by St. John of the Cross as follows: *conformity to Jesus Christ* by meditating on his life, by imitating his virtues, and by rejecting "every satisfaction offered to the senses which is not for God's honour and glory".[35] It is true that St. John of the Cross tends to express himself in negative terms, but there is no difference essentially between this and the positive urging of St. Teresa towards the ideal of becoming the slave of Jesus Crucified. Either way, self has to yield to the growing life of Christ in the soul.

It is while the soul is still immersed in the attractions of the world and the flesh, then, that the full rigour of asceticism is so important. Other "beginners" in the interior life may be brought to the prayer of the "divine tastes" (fourth mansion Quiet) almost immediately, and from there into the passive night of sense, through no apparent merit of their own.[36] Later, too, our Lord assists the soul with multiplied actual graces, even undertaking the greater part of the purification himself, and finally the soul may have its freedom restored. The motive behind this work is at all times positive, and if on occasion some lesser good has to be sacrificed, this is solely for the purpose of securing something better. At every stage, moreover, it is our personal love of Jesus Christ and subsequent desire to imitate him which ensures that the asceticism of the soul does not degenerate into self-destruction.

It is supposed, not infrequently, that the main purpose of the active night of sense is to predispose the soul for the experience of the passive night of sense (as if the former were necessarily incomplete without the latter); and this can give rise to many unwarranted feelings of inferiority in souls whom God is leading by the simple unitive way. In reality, those whom God brings speedily to the prayer of the "divine tastes" have not even had time wherein to practise those deep, strong virtues which characterize the soul in the acquired night of sense; and if one of these souls already deeply grounded in virtue were at length to be introduced by God into the supernaturally passive ways, clearly its progress through the different phases of purification would be proportionately rapid. We must say, then, that the purpose of the night of sense (whether actively acquired or passively endured) is to bring the appetites of the soul, both concupiscible and irascible, under the perfect control of reason enlightened by faith. Only thus can the necessary strength be maintained for the consistent practice of prayer and recollection. Only thus, in conjunction with prayer and the sacraments, can the soul's spirit of faith be genuinely intensified. As St. John of the Cross insists at the beginning of the *Spiritual Canticle*, the soul that would attain to the blessed Trinity through union with the Beloved "must go out from all things in will and affection, and enter into the profoundest recollection".[37] According to St. Teresa, "the chief point is that we should resolutely give him our heart for his own and should empty it of everything else, that he may take out or put in whatever he pleases. . . ."[38]

Now the soul's spirit of faith is the first and most important element in this search for the Beloved—not merely the *habit* of faith, infused at baptism and sustained through the grace of subsequent sacraments, but that living flame of the intelligence in its search for God, which is ever active, ever hungering and thirsting after truth, ever seeking to build itself up at the hands of our Lady in the strength and merits of Jesus Crucified. In the first book of the *Ascent*, as we have seen, St. John of the Cross teaches how the powers of the soul may be thoroughly grounded in Christ. In the second book, then, he explains everything that the soul can do, of its own initiative, to develop and perfect its spirit of faith in this life. This teaching is not meant to be restricted in the sense that the soul may later disregard it. On the contrary, it holds good throughout our entire earthly pilgrimage (no matter to what kind or degree of contemplation we may attain), but it does not become of practical use initially unless the soul has first taken steps to build itself up in Christ in the manner already indicated. Just as a plant without roots cannot grow, so will our spirit of faith come to nothing unless first it be grounded in the knowledge of the Crucified and in all the truths of our holy religion. Even where there is genuine difficulty from the beginning in using a discursive method during formal prayer time, the same ground must be covered in other ways, for example through spiritual reading and other forms of prayerful study. Progression in prayer, progression towards the hidden Beloved, that is what matters most to St. John of the Cross; for which reason, he is as careful that the soul should not abandon

meditation too soon as he is anxious for it to go forward un-
hindered when the necessary maturity can be discerned.[39] St.
Teresa tells us that we do well to keep silence when His Majesty
indicates his attentiveness to our petitions. "If, however, the
King makes no sign of listening or of seeing us, there is no need
to stand inert, like a dolt, which the soul would resemble if it
continued inactive."[40]

Sometimes the inability to meditate is due only to some
temporary cause, the precise nature of which may be difficult to
diagnose; sometimes it becomes a total and permanent impossi-
bility during any period of formal prayer; but the only thing that
really matters to St. John of the Cross is *the practical conduct* of
the soul under whatever circumstances it may happen to find
itself. According to its dispositions at any particular moment, so
let it act, given however that immediate detachment be practised
in regard to all accidental phenomena. This doctrine of pure faith
occupies the remainder of the second book of the *Ascent* and is
without parallel in the history of spirituality for its psychological
penetration and practical wisdom. Substantial union with God—
through perfect faith, hope and love towards Christ the mediator
—that is the ultimate aim of St. John of the Cross in directing
souls; also all the instructions given in the second book of the
*Ascent* are there to be applied, as occasion demands, no matter
whether the souls in question be "progressives" or "proficients"
or even relatively perfect. To enter upon the obscure night is no
guarantee of perseverance therein. Nature, however, is there to
be perfected, not destroyed by the supernatural principle; hence
the danger of employing natural methods of repression for the
memory and will. This supernatural principle concerns the union
by faith of the individual intelligence with Jesus Christ, and the
more deeply *personal* this union becomes, the more effectively
is the will of God made known to the soul, even in the smallest
details. Theological hope perfects the memory in proportion as

faith is already operative in the understanding, and the will too experiences a mysterious adjustment or modification of its values, again in proportion as fresh enlightenment has come to it through faith. If the teaching given in the first fifteen chapters of the third book of the *Ascent* is practised without reference to the background provided by the second book, and especially if a strong spirit of faith is not yet established in the soul of the would-be contemplative, serious mental or nervous imbalance is liable to ensue. The doctrine of St. John of the Cross must be studied as an integrated whole, directly related at all times to Jesus Christ, and interpreted in accordance with the teaching of the Church (which it presupposes). As the saint himself used to declare: "The greatest honour we can render unto God, is to serve him in evangelical perfection: and whatever is beside this, is of no value or advantage to man."[41]

We must also appreciate that certain principles of interior development remain constant, no matter by what path God leads the soul to the perfection of charity. When these are kept in mind, there is less danger of assuming that a soul in the obscure night is necessarily more excellent than one who retains the initiative in matters of prayer and the virtues. What counts in the eyes of God is the manner in which *we use* the particular talents and graces bestowed upon us, and none but he is in the position to compare the value for eternity of the labourers in his vineyard. Objectively speaking, it is true, union with God in this life is perfect in proportion as the entire soul is rendered Deiform, and to this end every soul in the state of grace may lawfully aspire. At the same time, however, we must recall the words of Abbot Blosius that the attainment of this desire may not be granted here below. God is the perfector of all his creatures, invariably working in accordance with the nature and circumstances of each, for which reason St. John of the Cross declares in the second book of the *Ascent:* "It is evident that God, when he elevates the soul from the depths of its own vileness to the opposite heights of his own dignity in union with himself, worketh orderly, sweetly and in harmony with the constitution of the soul."[42] As St. Teresa puts it: "Our Lord knows for what everybody is suited, and gives each one what is best for her soul, for his own glory, and for the good of her neighbour."[43]

In the twelfth to fourteenth chapters of the second book of the *Ascent*, St. John of the Cross makes it clear that the soul who has been inspired by the example of Jesus Christ, ordinarily arrives at a state of simple loving attention to his presence through prolonged exercise in meditation and the assiduous practice of all the virtues. In the centuries which followed, this kind of simple recollection was given the name of "spiritual contemplation" or "acquired contemplation", and when the connatural enjoyment of the will was also very marked, the term "infused contemplation" was used to describe its sequel. Outwardly, it would seem to be identical with the "active recollection" found in St. Teresa's third mansion, but when we examine closely what happens next, we soon discover that the Teresian recollection at this stage is nowhere near so strong or mature a phenomenon as at first supposed. In short, the Teresian recollection depends far more on simple affections and acts of the will than on the high-powered light of faith, which in theological minds is often the fruit of prolonged intellectual enquiry. The truth of this statement will become more apparent if we first state the Teresian view of the third mansion.

Of all St. Teresa's mansions, this third one strikes us as the least attractive. If the soul is able to get out of it quickly, great is its good fortune, but for very many people it seems to resemble more closely a penitentiary without any visible exit. Let us then see the main types of development which can here be observed. First, there is the type of soul who is destined to remain in this state for a very long time, perhaps for the greater part of its life, free from all deliberate sin, exemplary in outward behaviour, yet for one reason or another unable to make further progress. In this condition, the ability to make simple reflexions and aspirations in support of recollection is usually retained, but there may be long spells of aridity wherein the temptation to abandon the practice of prayer is very great. The possible causes of this aridity are manifold: physical, nervous or emotional tension, for example, psychological discouragement, faults of pride or attachment to self-will and private judgement on the spiritual plane, lack of generosity or community spirit, frustrated ambitions or spiritual envy. With each successive year, such habits become more difficult to combat, and as the soul concerned is often oblivious to them, they serve for the most part as occasions for fraternal charity in others. The arid experience in such cases is sometimes called obscure contemplation, in this context a kind of courtesy-title for the ills arising from our own human limitations; but although it bears certain resemblances to the infused prayer of that name, it is in fact a spiritual cul-de-sac out of which every possible effort should be made to escape. Sometimes, in fact, some unexpected lapse into actual sin is providentially necessary in order to rouse the soul from its self-complacency or secret pride. St. Teresa makes several penetrating observations about this interior state and warns her readers that the way of such souls "will be difficult and wearisome without self-renunciation, weighed down as we are by the burden and frailties of human nature, which are no longer felt in the more interior mansions".[44] Secondly, there is the case of the soul whose humility, fidelity and self-sacrifice is so marked that short spells of infused light and consolation are granted, usually of an affective or devotional nature, during which times the simple practice of the presence of God asserts itself quite easily. Both before and afterwards, however, such a soul usually regains its ability to make simple reflexions and aspirations in prayer, and feels more secure when thus engaged. Like a child venturing into deep water, it trusts itself to swim or float for short periods, but is always more at ease with its feet touching familiar ground, or at least within reach of that ground. "For the love of God," urges St. Teresa, "let us exert ourselves, and leave our reason and our fears in his hands, paying no attention to the weaknesses of nature which might retard us."[45] Thirdly, there is the case of the soul in whom recollection is so quickly and effectively intensified that she straightway resolves to abandon all things, in order to have greater fruition of her Beloved, and St. Teresa describes this beginning of infused recollection as a very great help and consolation. She adds, however, that no one should feel dismayed if it is withheld from them through no fault of their own, since His Majesty knows best how to distribute his gifts. This last point is of special importance, because in some cases the soul is brought from the recollection of the third mansion to the quiet of the fifth mansion *without* experiencing any of the infused delights peculiar to the fourth mansion, which normally precede the passive night of sense or prayer of obscure contemplation. Indeed, for the soul to enter the passive night of sense without previous elevations of the will to any marked degree, is common enough when genuine "acquired contemplation" has been practised instead. Common to both states is an intensified light of faith, even although the predisposing cause of this intensification differs according to the nature of the soul concerned. In practice, however, this light—in the Teresian experience— *dazzles* the mental eye before blinding it; whereas, in the case of the progressives of St. John of the Cross, the blinding process is more gradual and more gentle, less disturbing moreover to the general equilibrium of the soul. The meaning of this word "blinding" is explained by St. John of the Cross in the second book of the *Obscure Night* where he says that "the more clear and self-evident divine things are, the more obscure and hidden they are to the soul naturally", therefore that "the divine light of contemplation, when it shines into the soul . . . obscures it and deprives it of its natural perceptions".[46]

Now the only direct reference which St. John of the Cross makes to St. Teresa's fourth mansion is that which occurs in the first chapter of the first book of the *Obscure Night*, and it is quite clear that he is speaking—in this context— not of "progressives" but of the second variety of "beginners" in the night of sense. All the advantages of his obscure night are extolled by comparison, as it were, with these preceding degrees of subjective union in which the natural faculties and senses rejoice; and in the opening stanzas of the *Spiritual Canticle*, too, the preceding affective experience wherein the soul is "wounded" by the Beloved, is implied rather than described. Schooled in the objective outlook of the philosophers and theologians, St. John of the Cross shows a marked reluctance to dwell on the infused consolations which St. Teresa has described so vividly. To her, they were an indispensable source of fortitude in view of subsequent trials; to him, they were—at best—no more than a prelude to the vitally important night of sense and faith. Both points of view are in fact correct, though more damage is done by over-estimating than by under-estimating the value of this subjective contemplation which so often precedes the infused obscure night. Just as the human eye is not dazzled until it has looked upon the sun, and the human soul at death does not experience purgatory until it has looked upon God as he really is, so here the obscure night is *a contrast*, not merely with the soul's former ability to make discursive prayer or to contemplate the divine attributes, but more especially with the intermediate dilation of mind and heart peculiar to the fourth mansion, which serves so effectively to detach the memory from its circumscribed ways and natural fearfulness. Good Friday for Peter, for John and for James was preceded by the grace and mystery of the transfiguration on Mount Tabor. Our Lord, however, knows what is best for each of us, and St. Teresa is at one with St. John of the Cross in teaching that gratuitous favours should not be striven after. The imitation of our Lord is what really matters, also the determination to serve him without any thought of pleasing ourselves.

The phenomenon which St. John of the Cross calls "the passive night" is brought about exclusively by the infused light of faith in the natural understanding. This light, in itself, differs only in degree of intensity from that which the soul has already received (either by means of acquired contemplation or else gratuitously in the fourth mansion); but the *effect* of this light is now different because of the change taking place in the soul's dispositions. This change of disposition is intimately associated with the attainment of the soul to emotional maturity, together with the natural integration of self which can then be realized. For some people, this attainment is a relatively easy one; for others, and through no deliberate fault of their own, it may take a life-time. In short, the providence of God has a bigger part to play in this respect than do the virtues and the spirit of mortification, and in some cases it would almost seem as though providence had done everything. Entry into the passive night is in no sense a reward for merit; it simply means that the soul possesses the natural dispositions required for a life of child-like dependence on Jesus Christ. As we are, so does he perfect us; and it is the practice of virtue *in the circumstances wherein we are placed* that determines the less or more of our individual sanctity. Even amongst the canonized saints, relatively few—least of all in the olden days—appear to have been led by this wholly passive way. It is, however, of great advantage to the soul when God invites it thus to journey to him in pure faith. The psychological difference between the "three signs" of the obscure night and the three more elementary ones described in the *Ascent* should be

8

noted carefully. It is a mistake to suppose that the latter indicate greater perfection, even although the senses may testify to the contrary. Likewise, in the words of St. John of the Cross, "it is very foolish, when spiritual sweetness and delight fail, to imagine that God has failed us also".[47]

The faults and imperfections which St. John of the Cross deals with in the first seven chapters of the first book of *Obscure Night* are all associated directly with spiritual pride. Thus spiritual avarice, luxury and wrath, spiritual gluttony, envy and sloth, can all be traced back to the same poisonous root and represent the *particular* defects of the soul that has been raised above its ordinary condition by the gratuitous action of God at an early stage in its supernatural development. In the case of those who pass directly from acquired contemplation into the passive night (having practised all the virtues over a long period of time), it stands to reason that less purification will be required. The main difference, then, is this. Souls well tried in the practice of virtue already possess sufficient humility to respond to counsel from the confessor or superior; but with spiritual "beginners" this is not so. Correction is resented. Words of restraint go unheeded. The soul regards itself as misunderstood, even as a martyr, and complains bitterly that no one else is sufficiently enlightened to appreciate its own exalted perfection. God therefore has to intervene; and this he does by intensifying still further the infused light of his own presence, in such a way that the senses lose entirely their ordinary powers of apprehension during prayer-time, leaving the soul (as it were) in darkness and unknowing. This cure for spiritual pride and its secondary manifestations is indeed a drastic one, but it is the best possible antidote for the influence of the devil, which would otherwise gain the mastery. Nothing is more humbling than the inescapable fear of being lost on the road.

The two books of the *Obscure Night* will always seem

difficult to those who have no taste for abstract thought, also to those who have no first-hand experience of the interior helplessness involved. Just as a man who had been blinded suddenly in the prime of life might later write a book about the way in which this experience had affected him, so too does St. John of the Cross give us these brilliant psychological sketches of the progressive reactions of the soul to the infused light of faith. In modern times, St. Thérèse of Lisieux has translated this same teaching into the language of childhood, and some people find this easier to understand, supposedly at least. Objectively, however, our understanding of these deep things of God is always in the measure of our individual spirit of faith. However much we try to manipulate truth to suit our own conceptions, truth remains as it always has been, and always will be, inseparable from the Word of God.

The first part of the obscure night, if looked at positively, corresponds with the first eleven stanzas of the *Spiritual Canticle*, also with the Teresian prayer of the third water in which the predominating desire of the soul is to obtain deeper fruition of God. In the teaching of St. John of the Cross, three conditions for the realization of this fruition must be noted: first, God himself must be the principal agent in the work; secondly, the soul must remain faithful to the instruction laid down in the second book of the *Ascent;* thirdly, the soul must be conducted on the lines laid down in the tenth chapter of the first book of the *Obscure Night*. In short, "the soul should keep in mind that it is now making greater progress than it could make by any efforts of its own, though it be wholly unconscious of that progress, God himself is carrying it in his own arms . . . God himself is working".[48]

In the fourth stanza of the *Living Flame*, as we have seen, St. John of the Cross states that the "sweet embracing" of mystical union takes place in the deepest substance of the soul. As already noted, too, this is not the case in the forms of supernatural communication which the soul may experience before entering the obscure night. This distinction is important, because St. John of the Cross does not qualify directly the word "contemplation" for the purpose of showing the difference between the experience of the "progressives" and the experience of those whom the obscure night has rendered "proficient", and this is apt to cause confusion. Only in the *Spiritual Canticle* does the bride pray of set purpose "to see the face of God", this being " the essential communication of his divinity to the soul . . . something beyond sense and divested of accidents, inasmuch as it is the contact of pure substances, that is, of the soul and the divinity".[49]

Since this essential communication is something wholly secret and withdrawn from the knowledge of the senses, likewise from the comprehension of the understanding and even from the devil, it may be asked—not unreasonably—how it comes to be manifested to the conscious soul. At first sight, there would seem to be a contradiction in what has been said; yet the deeper meaning becomes apparent when we examine the teaching of St. John of the Cross on this point in greater detail. Thus in the fourteenth stanza of the *Spiritual Canticle* he writes: "The whisper of the gales is a most sublime and sweet understanding of God and of his attributes, which overflows into the intellect from the contact of the attributes of God with the substance of the soul"; and explaining this he says: "As the touch of the air is felt in the sense of touch, and the whisper of it heard in the ear, so also the contact of the virtues of the Beloved is felt and enjoyed in the touch of the soul, that is, in the substance thereof. . . . This divine whisper which enters in by the ear of the soul is not only substantial intelligence but a manifestation also of the truths of the divinity."[50] In the twenty-fifth stanza likewise, he explains that the touch or contact of fire "is that most delicate touch of the Beloved which the soul feels at times, even when least expecting it, and which is so penetrating that the heart is set on fire with love".[51] Already we begin to perceive three stages within the single grace bestowed: the *touch* itself, passively received within the substance of the soul; the *reflex communication*, through one of the spiritual senses, informing the understanding about the experience suffered; and the *overflow* of delight, to lesser or greater degree, into the conscious will. The intimacy of these touches varies considerably, however, and in the second book of the *Obscure Night* St. John of the Cross makes it clear that until the understanding has been fully prepared, "it is more common for the touch of the fire of love to be felt in the will than for the touch of the perfect intelligence to be felt in the intellect".[52] During the remainder of this thirteenth chapter, he develops and explains at length this distinction. In the twenty-sixth chapter of the second book of the *Ascent*, moreover, he sums up the difference between divine touches of knowledge and the vision of interior truths about things lower than God. Only the former pertain to substantial union. In regard to all else, the same rules of detachment as before must at all times be practised.

So far as the prayer of mystic Quiet and Union is concerned (the Teresian fifth mansion), the touches experienced are usually perceptible to the will only. Further purgation and the understanding becomes capable of hearing in a purely spiritual manner. Meantime, however, it must be understood with confidence that "if a soul is seeking after God, its Beloved is seeking it much more" and that when he wills him its loving desires . . . he on his part sends forth the odour of his ointments, which draw the soul and make it run after him".[53] Thus is the soul both elevated and purified whilst subject to the direct action of God. The benefits of the obscure night are summarized in the twelfth and thirteenth chapters of the first book, and then in the fourteenth chapter St. John of the Cross explains why the length and intensity of this purgation varies in different souls. After enumerating these possible variations of experience, he concludes by saying that the souls destined for the highest degrees of union are usually subject to aridity and temptations for a very long time "however quickly God may lead them".[54] As regards the difference between the "night of sense" and the "night of faith", St. John of the Cross explains this in the second chapter of the second book of the *Ascent*. In this pure infused faith, the soul is brought into the darkest part of the night; but one cannot say exactly where the new phase begins or ends, because—like midnight in relation to the gathering dusk and the gradual dawn—it is in fact continuous with the passive purifications of sense and spirit, provided of course that the soul perseveres in its humble co-operation with the divine initiative.

In the course of the obscure night, neither duties of state nor necessary conversation with others can interrupt the action of God, but it is indispensable that the soul be detached from all accidental phenomena and other supernatural apprehensions as detailed in the second book of the *Ascent*. If it be His Majesty's will to grant particular favours to the soul, especially those in the nature of visions and ecstasy, this detachment will not prove a hindrance; but it will on the other hand give protection against the devil and self-delusion, and that is why St. John of the Cross insists on maintaining the active night of faith until in heaven the beatific vision is attained. The soul that is led by the Spirit of God becomes increasingly aware of its natural frailty, and that is why it seeks the grace of substantial union only. The deeper purgation of the understanding and memory is described in the second book of the *Obscure Night*.

As regards the vocation to spiritual marriage, St. John of the Cross distinguishes between "the fruition of God by grace only" and "the fruition of him in union also", and he says that the difference between these two states "resembles that which exists between espousals and marriage". [55] The first involves "only an agreement and the mutual good will of the parties"; the second concerns also "personal union and mutual self-surrender".[56] The fourteenth to twenty-first stanzas of the *Spiritual Canticle* treat likewise of this blessed time of preparation for the marriage between the soul and her Spouse, the Son of God. Similar teaching, too, is given in the fourteenth chapter and following of the second book of the *Obscure Night*, but this is expressed in a more abstract manner. The seventeenth and eighteenth chapters speak of the secrecy of this dark contemplation, then of the secret wisdom or ladder which facilitates the ascent to God. The twenty-first chapter explains the meaning of the word "disguised" in relation to the understanding, memory and will; and in the two subsequent chapters, we realize yet again how blessed is the divine darkness which affords such protection against the jealous strategies of the devil. "Neither angel nor devil can discover what is going on" in the substance of the soul, neither can they interfere with these secret communications of the Lord, these "substantial touches of the divine union between himself and the soul",[57] because these are entirely his own work.

Concerning the graces which pertain to transforming union and spiritual marriage, St. John of the Cross remarks in the third stanza of the *Living Flame* that if the preliminary unctions of the Holy Spirit in the caverns of the soul are so sublime, it is even more difficult to do justice to their completion. Certainly this act of transformation in the soul is not so perfect as in the life to come, but "there is in fact a mutual interchange of love, between the soul and God in the conformity of their union, and in the matrimonial surrender wherein the goods of both, that is the divine essence, are possessed by both together in the voluntary giving up of each to the other".[58] It is not surprising, then, that the initial desire of the soul on attaining to this new Deiform life, should be for the completion of its hope in the beatific vision; and it is indeed to this end that the bride prays: "Break thou the slender web of this life that I may be enabled to love thee hereafter with that fulness and abundance which my soul desires, without end and for evermore."[59]

The teaching given in the *Spiritual Canticle*, although essentially the same as in the *Living Flame*, gives greater prominence to certain doctrinal points. In the first place, St. John of the Cross expresses the opinion that "no soul ever attains to this state without being confirmed in grace in it, for the faith of both is confirmed";[60] and again he speaks of "the union of the soul's strength, or, rather, of the soul's weakness, with the strength of God, in whom our weakness, resting and transformed, puts on the strength of God himself".[61] In the second place, St. John of the Cross stresses that this absorption of the soul in God is not to be understood in any pantheistic sense. The spouse of the soul is Jesus Christ, and it is only by virtue of the hypostatic union of his two natures that we can attain to his divinity. "The sweet mysteries of his Incarnation, the ways and means of redemption"[62] comprise the greater part of what he now communicates to the soul. Thirdly, in the twenty-sixth stanza, where St. John of the Cross refers to the different "cellars" of love or gifts of the Holy Ghost, it is interesting to note that he cites the gift of fear as the last and most perfect degree of participated love, consequently as the "cellar" wherein the spiritual marriage is consummated. Here, it must be noted, he is speaking of this gift in its perfection. The same gift, in its ordinary sense, has its special function at the beginning of the interior life. Fourthly, St. John of the Cross points out that although "the soul be always in the high estate of marriage ever since God has placed it there, yet *actual* union in all its powers is not continuous".[63] The substantial union with God abides, but the union of the faculties in the active sense "is not, and cannot be, permanent in this life".[64] It remains, then, to consider the apostolic value within the Church of these great favours, for sometimes the Word Incarnate has other plans for the soul than that of allowing her to proceed immediately to her heavenly reward.

As already observed, the soul in the state of spiritual betrothal, and also during the first stages of initiation into the spiritual marriage, is wholly taken up with the transfer to the Beloved of all her powers and possessions, virtues, gifts and above all her strength.[65] In the second paragraph of the introduction to the twenty-ninth stanza, for example, St. John of the Cross draws special attention to the value within the Church of this "pure love" as distinct from the works which may or may not proceed from it (subject to the divine will), and he again emphasizes this point in the subsequent paragraph. Is this in contradiction of St. Teresa's teaching about *works* being the purpose of spiritual marriage? Superficially, it might seem to be; yet in practice it is all a question of whether or not the will of the Beloved is *informing* the acts in operation. St. John of the Cross approaches the subject as the doctor of substantial union, to which fine needle-point all else is reduced. St. Teresa, on the other hand, simply takes it as *part* of her personal union with our Lord that she should be ready at all times to do his bidding, no matter at what cost to herself. It would be altogether wrong to suppose that the apostolic works of St. Teresa were not informed by the same "pure and solitary love" as that of which St. John of the Cross so eloquently speaks. At all times, too, the soul requires a measure of literal solitude for the balance of her interior powers, and this—like her works of love— is again regulated for her by the will of her Beloved. In the thirty-sixth stanza, then, we find the bride beginning to realize that the ultimate perfection of her transformation in the Son of God depends as much on her loving identification with the works of his redemption as on the deifying power of the consolations which she receives from him;

and therefore she prays to enter more deeply into the thicket of the Cross. This new phase of working and suffering in union with the Word Incarnate on behalf of his mystical body may extend over many years. It is true, however, that St. John of the Cross somewhat telescopes the point in his zeal to complete the descriptive range of the soul's unitive experience here on earth. Physically, moreover, he himself was severely reduced through imprisonment, malnutrition and excessive corporal sufferings, so it need not surprise us that his own thirst for the beatific vision should have been so great. We must repeat, then, that the works of the apostolate are only of value in so far as God has informed their spirit. Always—in the last analysis—it is the faith, hope and charity of the soul which has the real power over the Beloved and which draws from his Sacred Heart such unparalleled graces of union and spiritual fruition for the benefit of his mystical body as a whole.

The last four stanzas of the *Spiritual Canticle* are of exceptional beauty, and are concerned solely with the intimate relationship between the bride and her Spouse as she penetrates—ever more deeply—into the treasure-house of his mysteries, his wisdom and his eternal power within the Church. The language is akin to that used in the first and fourth stanzas of the *Living Flame*, and we can conjecture what might have been the saint's exposition of the last five stanzas of his poem, the *Obscure Night of the Soul*. All the writings of St. John of the Cross are as the pieces of one single jigsaw puzzle, one which might well be inscribed: THE BLESSED NIGHT OF FAITH; for, as love is to the garland of virtues within the soul, so to the human understanding is this light of pure faith, under every possible circumstance willed or permitted by the providence of God. It is worth remembering, however, that "the divinely wise and the worldly wise are fools in the estimation of each other"[66], also that God alone can open the eyes of the intellect to the sublime knowledge of himself. "In this union of the divine wisdom," St. John of the Cross explains, "it is the great light that shines overwhelming the less, yet the latter is not therefore lost, but rather perfected, though it be not the light which shines pre-eminently."[67] Happy is the man who is content to occupy this second place in the divine economy.

[1]Pourrat, Vol. 2, p. 336.
[2]Pourrat, Vol. 3, pp. 1–79.
[3]*Book of Spiritual Instruction*, p. 66.
[4]*Obscure Night of the Soul II*, 17, 4; p. 428, Vol. 1, L. G. & Co., 1864.
[5]Pourrat, Vol. 3, pp. 80–123.
[6]See Part Two, p. 53.
[7]A Franciscan martyr, author of *Blanquerna*, a mystical romance.
[8]Tercer. Abeced. trat. xxi; see Pourrat, p. 91.
[9]An Andalusian lay-brother, author of *The Ascent of Mt. Sion.*
[10]Cf. *Way of Perfection*, Ch. 18.3; and Ch. 25.1.
[11]*Living Flame*, III, line 3, para. 5; p. 267, Vol. 2, L. G. & Co.
[12]See *Way of Perfection*, Ch. 28.
[13]See *Interior Castle*, Mansion 4.3.
[14]Spiritual Maxim, No. 274; p. 378, Vol. 2, L. G. & Co.
[15]*Interior Castle*, Mansion 4.3; p. 114, Baker.
[16]See also *Book of Foundations*, Ch. 6.
[17]*Way of Perfection*, Ch. 31; p. 180, Baker.
[18]p. 393, Vol. 2, L. G. & Co.
[19]*Interior Castle*, Mansion 5.1.8; p. 125, Baker.
[20]Loc. cit., p. 128, Baker.
[21]*Interior Castle*, Mansion 5.4.
[22]*Living Flame*, IV, line 3; p. 302, Vol. 2, L. G. & Co.
[23]*Living Flame*, IV, line 3; pp. 303–4, Vol. 2, L. G. & Co.
[24]Stanza 13; p. 70, Vol. 2, L. G. & Co.
[25]*Interior Castle*, Mansion 6.1; p. 162, Baker.
[26]p. 67, Vol. 2, L. G. & Co.
[27]*Living Flame*, III, line 3.3; p. 265, Vol. 2, L. G. & Co.
[28]*Interior Castle*, Mansion 7.2.2. & 3; p. 271, Baker.
[29]Loc. cit., p. 272, Baker.
[30]*Interior Castle*, Mansion 7.3.8; p. 282, Baker.
[31]*Spiritual Canticle*, XXXIV; p. 180, Vol. 2, L. G. & Co.
[32]*Interior Castle*, Mansion 7.4.9; p. 289, Baker.
[33]*Interior Castle*, Mansion 7.4.13; p. 291, Baker.
[34]*Ascent I*, 11.3; p. 40, Vol. 1, L. G. & Co.
[35]*Ascent I*, 13.4; p. 48, Vol. 1, L. G. & Co.

[36]See *Ascent I*, 13.1 also *Obscure Night I*, 3.
[37]*Spiritual Canticle*, 1; p. 16, Vol. 2, L. G. & Co.
[38]*Way of Perfection*, Ch. 28, 12; p. 165, Baker.
[39]See *Ascent II*, 13–15.
[40]*Interior Castle*, Mansion 4.3; pp. 110–1, Baker.
[41]Spiritual Maxim, No. 199; p. 369, Vol. 2, L. G. & Co.
[42]*Ascent II*, 17.2; p. 123, Vol. I, L. G. & Co.
[43]*Way of Perfection*, Ch. 18.1; p. 102, Baker.
[44]*Interior Castle*, Mansion 3.2; p. 83, Baker.
[45]*Interior Castle*, Mansion 3.2; pp. 82–3, Baker.
[46]*Obscure Night of the Soul II*, 5.3; p. 381, Vol. 1, L. G. & Co.
[47]Spiritual Maxim, No. 240; p. 373, Vol. 2, L. G. & Co.
[48]*Living Flame*, III, line 3, para. 16; p. 287, Vol. 2, L. &. & Co.
[49]*Spiritual Canticle*, XIX. 2; p. 106, Vol. 2, L. G.& Co.
[50]*Spiritual Canticle*, XIV, line 5; pp. 80–7, Vol. 2, L. G. & Co.
[51]*Spiritual Canticle*, XXV, line 3; p. 133, Vol. 2, L. G. & Co.
[52]*Obscure Night of the Soul II*, 13.1; p. 412, Vol. 1, L. G. & Co.
[53]*Living Flame*, III, line 3, para. 4; p. 266, Vol. 2, L. G. & Co.
[54]*Obscure Night of the Soul I*, 14.8; p. 372, Vol. 1, L. G. & Co.
[55]*Living Flame*, III, line 3, para. 3; p. 264, Vol. 2, L. G. & Co.
[56]Loc. cit.
[57]*Obscure Night of the Soul II*, 23, 10; p. 451, Vol. 1, L. G. & Co.
[58]*Living Flame*, III, line 6; p. 294, Vol. 2, L. G. & Co.
[59]*Living Flame*, I, line 6; p. 235, Vol. 2, L. G. & Co.
[60]*Spiritual Canticle*, XXII; p. 119. Vol. 2, L. G. & Co.
[61]Loc. cit., p. 122, Vol. 2, L. G. & Co.
[62]Loc. cit., p. 123, Vol. 2, L. G. & Co.
[63]Stanza XXVI; p. 141, Vol. 2, L. G. & Co.
[64]Loc. cit., p. 142; cf. Part 2, para. 49.
[65]See Stanzas XXVI–XXXV.
[66]*Spiritual Canticle*, XXVI; p. 143, Vol. 2, L. G. & Co.
[67]Loc. cit., p. 144.

## PART FOUR

# THE EFFECTS OF CHRISTIAN HUMANISM ON MYSTICAL THEOLOGY

## FOREWORD

IN ALL her writings, St. Teresa of Avila never failed to urge her readers towards the perfection of charity, but she always made it clear that this perfection could neither be attained nor preserved by love alone, not even by prayer and contemplation alone. In short, an interior foundation for the Spirit of God to work upon is indispensable—a foundation of virtue, of self-knowledge and of good practical sense—also, at every stage of interior development, the consistent practice of certain virtues in particular is necessary for the protection of the soul's gifts. These virtues are: *faith* in prayer and the Rule, in divine providence, and in the nearness of Jesus and Mary at all times to help us in our difficulties; *hope* in the divine promises and in the power of sacramental grace, aided by true poverty of spirit in regard to all else; *charity* as proved by fraternal love and readiness to sacrifice self for the greater good of another; *prudence* in the exercise of charity and apostolic zeal; *obedience* in accordance with one's state in life; *humility* and *openness* in all dealings with those representing our Lord in our regard, offset however by real magnanimity of purpose. If any of these qualities are defective, the soul will become aware of threatened disturbance in regard to its inner tranquillity of spirit. Ideally then, as St. John of the Cross writes in the last stanza of the *Spiritual Canticle:* "The practice of virtue and the state of perfection to which the soul has come, is a victory over Satan, and causes him such terror that he cannot present himself before it."[1]

It is sometimes asserted that contemplative nuns live in selfish ignorance of the cares of the outside world, but certainly in the case of St. Teresa she was fully alive to the sinful state of Europe by the mid-sixteenth century. Although, too, the entire work of her Reform was dedicated to the salvation of those countless souls who seemed bent on self-destruction, she knew that her deepest aspirations could only be realized through the clergy, above all through her own spiritual sons, the Fathers of the Reform, according as they were trained in the ways of true spirituality. In temperament, St. Teresa and St. John of the Cross made an interesting contrast, but because they were both so profoundly immersed in the mystery of Christ and in devotion to his Sacred Humanity, so in him did they flower together for the glory of the Church and the practical instruction of future generations. Three hundred years were to elapse before a work of parallel comprehensiveness was destined to be written, namely the *Story of a Soul* by St. Thérèse of Lisieux. Meantime, certainly, infused contemplation is ably described in relation to the transformation of the will, but not in relation to the transformation of the understanding and memory by pure faith and hope. After the seraphic outpourings of the Italian reformers, moreover, the theologians and mystical writers are gradually caught up in the cross-currents of Jansenism and Quietism (the reactionary exaggerations ultimately born of sixteenth-century humanism in Italy and France), and their writings are a faithful mirror of the world in which they lived. After every flowering of a plant or tree, there is a short period of glory, then the strength of the organism is withdrawn into the roots and into the central stem or trunk. Just so, in the life of the Church, there has to be a constant renewal of its fundamental strength and dogmatic awareness as contained in the Deposit of Faith, and this is what took place following the ravages of the Protestant Reformation. Mystical writings at the time were as apple-blossom after a hailstorm, and for most Christians their deeper meaning remained entirely veiled.

## 1 SPANISH MYSTICISM IN THE LATE SIXTEENTH AND SEVENTEENTH CENTURIES

The writings of the Spanish theologians became prolific at this time, and Pourrat gives a list of some eighteen of the principal treatises on mystical themes.[2] The real cause of this intense discussion was the baffling nature of "perfect contemplation" as envisaged by St. John of the Cross and by St. Teresa in the last three mansions of her *Interior Castle;* but even at the end of it all, the learned men do not seem to have been much further forward. The reason perhaps is this. The contemplation of St. John of the Cross's "progressives" could be understood easily enough by the educated Christian mind at that period, and even the infused contemplation given to the will in varying degrees could be explained by the Thomist laws of connaturality; but any idea of intellectual *passivity* was not only anathema to the metaphysicians, it was also the object of deep suspicion for the heresy-hunters. St. Teresa, as we have seen, warned people continually about the danger and stupidity of trying to place themselves in a passive state, but her counsel was otherwise when God himself took the initiative, either suspending the powers (as in affective union or ecstasy) or, by ligature, causing the natural operations of the understanding and memory to cease. Quietism is a state produced by the *deliberate* suppression of the acts of the powers, leading as often as not to the infusion of illuministic feelings and impressions by the devil, and that is where the danger lies. Nevertheless, the Jesuit theologian

Suarez declared that "no mode of prayer can be imagined in which the understanding and will would be absolutely passive";[3] and, to many people, that statement has always seemed unanswerable.

A second school of mystical thought at this time was ready to concede the need for intellectual passivity, but insisted on the continued activity of the will. In this sort of contemplation, the soul had to maintain itself by acts of love, and although knowledge might be present at the beginning of mystical prayer, love alone remained afterwards. Alvarez de Paz, S.J. (1560–1620), seems to have been the principal writer on this type of affective contemplation, the summit of which resembled the vision of Moses and St. Paul, and in all he was able to distinguish fifteen degrees of ordinary and extraordinary mystical perfection, as distinct from contemplation in its more elementary form to which all might aspire. He agreed that discursive prayer or meditation was necessary for beginners, but only until such time as the heart had caught fire and the mind was capable of remaining in the divine presence without recourse to reasoning. St. Alphonsus Rodriguez (1531–1617), on the other hand, looked upon the experimental presence of God as an intellectual grace, and claimed that it intensified through suffering and ecstasy to a point resembling the beatific vision. Suarez considered that the intuitive vision of God might occur unaccompanied by ecstasy,[4] since this was so in the case of our Lord. However, for those to whom God did not grant extraordinary favours, the spiritual Exercises of St. Ignatius were held to be wholly sufficient.

The principal Discalced Carmelite writers at this time were: Ven. John of Jesus Mary (1564–1615), Fr. Thomas of Jesus (1564–1627), and Fr. Joseph of the Holy Spirit (d. 1674). All were concerned profoundly with the distinction between "acquired contemplation" and "infused contemplation", also with the question of precision as regards terminology, but the scope of their writings does not seem to go beyond the degrees of affective union or transformation of the will. The rest appears to have remained hidden from them. A second Fr. Joseph of the Holy Spirit (d. 1739) became the author of the famous logical synthesis of mysticism entitled *Cursus theologiae mystico-scolasticae* which was published in Seville.

## 2 THE SIXTEENTH CENTURY ITALIAN SCHOOL AND ITS CHARACTERISTICS

An interesting and very good example of the spirituality of Alvarez de Paz, S.J., was that of St. Mary Magdalen de' Pazzi, the famous ecstatic of the Calced Carmelite convent in Florence. Her principal director seems to have been the Jesuit, Virgil Cepari, and she made the Exercises of St. Ignatius regularly. Focusing her attention on the mystery of the blessed Trinity as revealed by the Word Incarnate, she studied carefully the writings of St. Augustine and St. Bernard, also to some extent St. Thomas, and then in ecstasy reproduced the doctrine in her own words. One ecstasy at the age of eighteen lasted for eight days, another the following year lasted for four days and four nights, and on this latter occasion "God told her to write to the Pope and to the cardinals beseeching them to work for the reform of the Church".[5] As many as six nuns at a time used to occupy themselves in writing, checking and listening to the ecstatic utterances, until finally "it became impossible to record everything".[6] Best known were the letters and other exhortations to high ecclesiastics, whom she believed it to be her mission to instruct and reprimand, but these communications were not always delivered as intended. A Dominican contemporary, St. Catherine de Ricci, believed herself to be entrusted with a similar

9

responsibility, and was treated with great respect by those whom she addressed: cardinals and bishops, superiors of religious orders and princes alike.

If it is difficult nowadays to appreciate the reforming methods adopted by the ecstatics, no less difficult is it to visualize the social conditions of the time, the immorality that existed on every side, and the luxury in which so many ecclesiastics were accustomed to live whilst neglecting their churches, the sick and the poor. Illiteracy was another problem, likewise the absence of religious instruction for the poor. Under such conditions, then, one would hardly expect to find a continued flowering of the spirituality of St. Teresa and St. John of the Cross. The perfection of charity was still the ideal, but charity had to begin its work at a much more humble level. As Pourrat remarks: "The Christian humanists of the peninsula dreamed of a religion 'wholly of art and charity, of beauty and love'. The optimistic calm and joyous rhythm of Raphael belong much more to their spirit than does the pessimism of Michael Angelo."[7] Platonism assured them that the human soul could expand indefinitely under the influence of divine love, and they delighted to discourse upon this theme.

Left to itself, like all other forms of naturally-inspired idealism, this humanistic outlook would soon have deteriorated. Underneath, however, an exceedingly vigorous type of spirituality was at work, one that was bent on the renewal of Christian life amongst the clergy, on the vanquishing of heresy, on the founding of schools and hospitals, and on the raising of moral standards everywhere. For these purposes, then, two kinds of Clerks Regular came into existence: those concerned with the reform of the clergy and the morals of the people; and those occupied with teaching and nursing.

Best known in the first group were the Theatines of St. Cajetan, the Oblates of St. Charles Borromeo, and the Oratorians of St. Philip Neri. Then the Fathers of Christian Doctrine, the Fathers of the Pious Schools, and the Ursuline Sisters of St. Angela Merici did most in the field of education. A humanistic secret society known as the Oratorio del Divino Amore (founded by a disciple of St. Catherine of Genoa, Ettore Vernazza) undertook the foundation of hospitals and other works of mercy, and St. Cajetan was one of the first to associate himself with this movement. The interior ideals of the time are best summed up in the Exercises of St. Ignatius and in a book attributed to the Theatine Father, Laurence Scupoli, entitled *The Spiritual Combat*. The emphasis here is almost exclusively on the rôle of sanctified will-power against the forces of evil, and the corresponding ideal in mystical circles was to experience a change or transformation of heart through the intensity of divine charity. The Franciscans, too, developed a marked attraction for the experience of infused light, the same kind of super-eminent experience as desired by the Platonists, and this gave rise to many commentaries on the teaching of St. Dionysius the Areopagite. The writings of St. Robert Bellarmine, S.J., were deeply affective, also Claud Acquaviva as General of the Society settled the conflicting claims of asceticism and mysticism by urging his subjects to concentrate on the Exercises of St. Ignatius—without however presuming to interfere with the liberty of those whom God chose to lead by the extraordinary mystical ways. St. Cajetan, St. Philip Neri, St. Aloysius Gonzaga, St. Catherine of Genoa, Blessed Osanna de Andreassi (Dominican) and Blessed Battista (Poor Clare) were as outstanding as the saints already mentioned for their seraphic ardours. St. Camillus de Lellis devoted his life to the care of the sick, and St. Jerome Emiliani to the education of orphans. As St. Angela Merici used to say: "It is charity which leads all to honour God and to help souls."[8]

## 3  St. Francis of Sales and His Spiritual Teaching

In the person and writings of St. Francis of Sales we find a unique combination of natural and supernatural qualities, optimism, gentleness and extraordinary personal charm. Most outstanding of all was the skill wherewith he gave interior direction to souls living in the world, also—for one so deeply affective—his great distrust of extraordinary mystical phenomena. Divine love was his aim but not to the exclusion of the rôle of faith and hope here below; and although after his death his teaching about holy indifference came to be interpreted in a quietistic sense, the self-oblivion of which he speaks is a *gift* of God rather than an attitude deliberately practised, in other words, an habitual *effect* of charity in the soul rather than a pious aspiration. Before we can serve God truly, we must learn to love him and to find out what he really wants of us. St. Francis of Sales has a wonderful sense of supernatural justice, and therefore he says: "The practice of devotion must be accommodated to the strength, to the affairs, and to the duties of each individually. . . . Devotion when it is true never spoils anything, but rather perfects all things, and when it becomes inconsistent with the lawful vocation of anyone it is certainly false."[9] This attitude to devotion also reflects closely the teaching of St. Thomas,[10] and it links up with the effective ideal of the Italian *Oratorio del Divino Amore*, but one would not think to associate it with anyone other than St. Francis of Sales himself, possibly because he was the first to make virtue attractive from the social standpoint and the practice of mortification so strictly interior.

Although trained by the Jesuits in Paris and in Padua, St. Francis of Sales was fully a Thomist in his attitude to the work of grace; and although he owed so much to the inspiration of St. Augustine of Hippo, he was never pessimistic about man and his fallen nature. For him, the supreme reality is the effective power of Christ to restore all things according to the will of the Father, and in this we find that he had much in common with St. Teresa.

As regards the foundation of Salesian mysticism, this is undoubtedly Ignatian with strong insistence on the humble virtues, on devotion to the Sacred Humanity, on distrust of the extraordinary, and on regular preparation for mental prayer. Later, as divine love begins to gain the ascendancy, St. Francis of Sales speaks of two parts of the reasonable soul, its *spirit* and its *sense*, the will being supreme over all. In this spirit or higher part of the reasonable soul, moreover, he distinguishes the sphere of intellectual activity from the actual seat of the theological virtues, and he defines the latter part as "a certain eminence and supreme point of the reason and spiritual faculty, which is not led by the light of argument or reasoning, but by a simple view of the understanding and a simple feeling of the will by which the mind acquiesces and submits to the truth and will of God".[11] Further, he compares this apex of the spirit to the sanctuary of Solomon's temple saying:—

> In the sanctuary, there were no windows to give light; in this degree of the mind, there is no enlightenment from discourse. In the sanctuary, all light entered through the door; in this degree, nothing enters into the mind except by faith, which produces, like rays, the sight and the sense of the beauty and goodness of the good pleasure of God. None entered the sanctuary but the High Priest; in this apex of the soul, discourse has no access, but only the great, universal and sovereign feeling that the divine will must be supremely loved, approved and embraced. . . .[12]

It is interesting to compare this teaching with that of the Cistercians on the *memoria*, also with the descriptions given by Blosius in the twelfth chapter of his *Book of Spiritual Instruction*.

Are we then to understand that St. Francis of Sales attained
to the same transformation of soul as did St. Teresa and St. John
of the Cross ? This seems probable, though his actual writings
do not prove the point conclusively and many details are withheld from our observation. The testimony given by St. Jane
Frances of Chantal in her deposition at the beatification process
provides the best evidence on this point. Speaking of his gift of
faith, she says that this was accompanied by "great clearness,
certainty, relish and an extraordinary sweetness". Further, she
declares that "with simple sight, he saw the truths of faith and . . .
subjected his understanding to these truths with an absolute
peace of mind and will". He called the place where these "clear
visions" took place "the sanctuary of God, where nothing enters
but the soul alone with its God".[13]

## 4   THE FRENCH SCHOOL

During the first part of the seventeenth century in France, St.
Francis of Sales exercised a deep influence over the spirituality
of the age, both personally and through the medium of his
writings. This influence was never predominant, however, and
in order to estimate the strength and the weakness, the glory and
the exaggeration of the famous French School, we have to look
first to the spreading popularity of the Ignatian *Spiritual Exercises*,
secondly to Cardinal de Bérulle and the Oratory of Jesus founded
in 1611. Another independent spiritual writer was Cardinal
Richelieu whose *Treatise on Christian Perfection* was first
published, after his death, in 1646.

Cardinal Richelieu, it is said, had the highest regard for the
French Oratory, yet there is nothing Berullian about his own
spirituality. His solicitude for the duties of one's state recalls St.
Francis of Sales; his insistence on mental prayer and on perfect

conformity to God's will has a Teresian flavour; and his theory of knowledge is distinctly Thomist. He distinguished two kinds of mental prayer: ordinary meditation and extraordinary contemplation. By contemplation, however, he understood—quite simply—divine enlightenment according to one of the three following ways: by the infusion of intelligible species, which are not drawn from the senses but formed by God *expressly* in the mind of man; by the infusion of a very powerful extraordinary light, whereby the soul knows God in a manner exceeding its ordinary strength; or by the passing light of glory, as in the case of Moses and St. Paul. Here, the influence of the sixteenth-century Jesuit school is uppermost.

The glory and strength of the French Oratory lies in its devotion to the mystery of the hypostatic union, its weakness in the exaggerated disparagement of fallen man which affects every theological conclusion reached like a distorting shadow. Cardinal de Bérulle himself desired that man should regard his soul "as the most vile and useless creature of all, nay, as dust, mud and a mass of corruption",[14] and his disciples in turn seemed to vie with one another in perpetuating the pessimistic view of the ravages caused by original sin. To some extent, the teaching of St. Augustine and even of St. Paul has been held responsible for this disfiguring gloom, but one must also regard it as an historical swing of the pendulum following the exaltation of human nature for its own sake, as found during the Renaissance in France and Italy. Further, Ignatian spirituality laid the whole burden of co-operation with sufficient grace on the human will, so that man and his failure to live up to the ideals required of him was constantly being deplored by the exponents of the interior life. De Bérulle in his first published work, *Brief Discours de l'Abnégation Intérieure*, made two demands: first, "a very low estimate of all created things and of oneself above all, acquired by the frequent thought of their baseness and by the daily experience of one's nothingness and infirmity"; secondly, "a very high idea of God, not by a high insight into the attributes of the divinity, which is not necessary and which few have; but by the total submission of self to God, in order to adore him, and give all power over us and what is ours, without reserving any personal interest however sacred".[15] By the time he had written his twelve famous discourses on the *Grandeurs de Jésus*, de Bérulle's basic themes—as stated above—had developed almost beyond recognition. From now on, his preoccupation is with the Word Incarnate, whose human nature—being stripped of its own personality—is "essentially in a state of servitude, and remains in this state, permanent and perpetual with regard to the divinity, by its own nature and condition".[16] Our Lady too, of course, is regarded as being in this state of servitude by reason of her intimate relationship with the God-man. St. Louis Grignion de Montfort ultimately perpetuated de Bérulle's "Vow of Servitude to Jesus and Mary", which at first gave rise to such controversy. De Bérulle's concept of the Incarnation as "the centre to which are related all things in the world of nature, of grace and of glory", likewise of the acts of Christ as "divinely human and humanly divine", and of "the incomparable love of God for us" thus manifested[17] is all beyond reproach. He died, we are told, on 2nd October 1629 while celebrating a votive Mass of the Incarnation before a picture of that same mystery.[18] The historians of the Oratory have no praise too high for their saintly and honoured father,[19] but there is little enough in this to throw further light on the principles already mentioned. Certainly the metaphysicians of the Sorbonne had made men forgetful of the living Jesus and his reign in souls, but the Church was in full possession of her Christological doctrines centuries before Pierre de Bérulle came to be regarded as a unique spiritual Copernicus. The exaggerations in his doctrine, moreover, were to have serious consequences in the years to come.

For de Bérulle, then, our Lord was "the true Sun towards which the earth and our hearts ought to be continually moving . . . the Sun of our souls whence they receive all grace, light and influence".[20] Philosophically, however, he remained a Platonist, and to some extent he made self-renunciation the *condition* of perfect union with Christ, rather than the *effect* of our union with him in living faith and hope. He safeguarded the principle of human freedom, but placed the efficacy of divine grace in a position of greater prominence. Thus Berullian abnegation consisted of three types of nothingness: that whence we were drawn by God at creation; that in which Adam has placed us by original sin; and that into which we must enter in order to be made one with Christ. Father de Condren, the second director of the Oratory, developed the first concept, associating it especially with the priesthood; Olier continued the theme by deploring the corruption and evil tendencies of the flesh; and de Bérulle himself discoursed on the third nothingness, preaching the annihilation of the natural soul in order that the Spirit of Jesus might take complete possession of it. "Jesus is all, and ought to be all in us," he said, "and we ought to be nothing, to treat ourselves as nothing, to be nothing in ourselves and have our being only in him. As we are by him and not by ourselves, so also we should be for him and not for ourselves. This is what we should begin on earth that it may be finished in heaven, where Jesus Christ will be all in all. This is the perfection to which it becomes us to aspire."[21] The connexion between this teaching and the French prayer of simple regard will be seen more clearly later.

The extreme pessimism of M. Olier can be accounted for in part by his own extraordinary sufferings of a neurotic character, and there is no doubt that many of his later writings reveal to us the teaching of the French school at its best. He stresses, for example, that at the moment of the Incarnation "Our Lord

consecrated himself entirely to the Father, himself and all his
members. . . . . He continues ever to live with the same dispositions that he had during his whole life; he never interrupts them
and ever offers himself, in himself and in all his members, to
God in all those circumstances in which they ought to serve him,
honour him and glorify him".[22] Father de Condren, on the
other hand, devotes himself to the consideration of the interior
annihilation and total immolation which constitute the victim
state or perpetual sacrifice of Jesus Christ, a sacrifice which lasts
"all his life from the first moment of the Incarnation until
eternity",[23] and makes of the heavenly phase a kind of synthesis
of all that has gone before.[24] In the late nineteenth century, we
find this eucharistic theory (which excludes the Thomist view
of the Sacrament-Sacrifice) being championed once more by M.
Lepin in his famous treatise, and many would like to see it as
part of the dogma of the Church. Any attempt to evaluate it
should also take into account the exaggerated views about
original sin which led so many theologians to despise, not only
their own bodies, but even the divine flesh and blood of our
Redeemer prior to his resurrection and ascension into heaven.

As might be expected, the view taken by the French Oratory
of the priesthood is a very exalted one—leaving, however, a
dangerous vacuum between the professed nothingness of the
creature and the sacerdotal dignity presented to the world. To
live as though nature had ceased to exist is far less humiliating
than the humble acceptance of that nature with a view to progressive sanctification; but—as Pourrat observes—"the French
School views the priesthood first of all from the standpoint of
Christ rather than of ourselves",[25] that is to say, from the
standpoint of the heavenly Christ. The mode of existence
peculiar to our Lord's sacramental life does not come into the
picture.

## 5 JANSENISTIC REACTIONS TO CHRISTIAN HUMANISM

One of the greatest advantages of Berullian spirituality was the impetus given to eucharistic devotion, one of its greatest drawbacks the encouragement which it afforded to the Jansenistic movement. Thus the Feast of the Heart of Jesus, which was celebrated for the first time in October 1672 in the Congregation of St. John Eudes, had its origin in the Berullian Feast of Jesus and in the Sulpician Feast of the Interior of Jesus. It was not until December of the following year that the first revelation concerning the Sacred Heart was granted to St. Margaret Mary at Paray-le-Monial. Significantly, however, differences of opinion soon arose as to what the term "Heart of Jesus" implied. "In the God-man," wrote St. John Eudes, "we adore three hearts which are only one same heart. . . . The first heart of the God-man is his corporal heart, *which is deified*, as are all the other parts of his sacred body, through the hypostatic union they have with the divine person of the Eternal Word. The second is his spiritual heart. . . . The third is his divine heart . . . three hearts in this wonderful God-man which are but one heart."[26] The concept of devotion to our Lord's corporal heart was largely repudiated, as might be expected, and the divine heart was regarded as synonymous with the Holy Spirit. Thus the symbolic and Berullian idea of a spiritual heart came to be preferred, typifying the very person of Christ, also "the higher part of his soul, with all the natural and supernatural perfections which are contained in it, such as its natural faculties, the memory, the understanding and the will, the plenitude of grace and virtue with which it was crowned, and the wonderful life of which it is the principle".[27] St. Margaret Mary, on the other hand, regarded the Sacred Heart with all the realism of a loving child. Why be concerned to spiritualize that which is already divine? That is the point so often overlooked in learned works.

Pourrat defines Jansenism as "an anti-dogmatic and anti-mystical reaction".[28] It had its origins in the controversy between Pelagius and St. Augustine, indeed even before that in the exaggerations manifested during the first three centuries of the Christian era, but more particularly in the conflict between the respective claims of nature and grace. The Augustinian view, as we have seen, tended to exaggerate the effect of original sin on men's passions; but this was corrected by St. Thomas Aquinas in his famous treatise on sin. The Christian humanists then completed the attitude that man's natural qualities were there to be cultivated; but it did not occur to them that these qualities, for all their natural excellence, still required to be *subordinated* to the supernatural principle, in order that they might be used in the direct service of Jesus Christ only, according to his wishes as manifested by divine providence, but not otherwise. Thus was developed the sin of intellectual pride or self-sufficiency in those who had acquired a certain degree of moral perfection. Surely if *the will* was operating in union with God, one could do as one pleased ? In practice, then, neither side in the controversy seems to have been alive to the Pauline doctrine that "the creature was made subject to vanity, not willingly, but by reason of him that made it subject, in hope" (Romans viii. 20)—hence the extreme bitterness of the conflict concerning the practical role of hope in balancing the interior life. Presumption no less than pessimism brings its own train of evil.

Visibly, the dogmatic storm first broke in the persons of Michael Baius (d. 1589) and Leonard Lessius, S.J. (d. 1623), the former a chancellor of the University of Louvain, the latter one of the professors.[29] Baius, whose errors were condemned in 1567 and 1579, taught that a rigid predestination to eternal loss held prisoner the souls of the unjustified, so that the only freedom they had was to sin still further. Lessius, on the other hand, held that every man was offered sufficient grace for his conversion, but that its *efficacy* depended on the individual will. As for pre-destination, it was to be understood in terms of the divine prevision of man's actual merit or demerit. Many opposed this teaching on the grounds that it was contrary to St. Augustine and St. Thomas Aquinas, but St. Francis of Sales for one gave it his open support, especially as regards the divine prevision of merits. Lessius made a deep study of the divine attributes, in order to prepare himself to teach this doctrine with greater authority, and in the preface to his subsequent treatise he included the following noteworthy statement about speculative theology in general:—

> This part of theological science is not only very consoling when one gets to know it well, but it can also lead to high perfection and great holiness. It is not of use simply for discussions in the schools, as some wrongly suppose; it can also do much for the spiritual benefit of each one of us. These theological considera-tions can raise the soul to God and enable us to contemplate, wonder at, worship, fear, praise and bless him; they keep us in his presence and help us more perfectly to conform our life to his good pleasure. That is the purpose of speculative theology.[30]

Thus love is the fulfilment of the soul, but knowledge under-stood in this way contributes to the fulfilment, even giving rise to mystical contemplation. In practice, a loving consideration of the divine attributes and perfections is always the main charac-teristic of acquired contemplation or the true prayer of simplicity.

In Spain, the dogmatic argument continued in the persons of Dominico Banez, O.P. (d. 1604), and Luis Molina, S.J. (d. 1601). Banez considered predestination as anterior to all prevision of merits, taking the line that man can only do freely that which God has decreed from all eternity. Molina, on the contrary, put the prevision of merits first, and made predestation depend on precisely that prevision. Neither view was checked by Pope

Paul V, but Molinism was dominant by the end of the sixteenth century, thereafter leading to the Augustinian reaction, which in turn went to the extreme of Jansenism.

Amongst those who reacted most strongly against the teaching of Molina was Cardinal de Bérulle. Augustinism for him was a much better instrument for accentuating the results of original sin, for emphasizing the nothingness of man in relation to God, for insisting on the sovereignty of grace, and for insisting that reliance on this grace was far more important than personal effort. When interpreted too literally, this Berullian doctrine has regrettable consequences. Meantime, however, de Condren, Olier, St. Vincent de Paul and St. John Eudes are all said to have been in support of the Thomist doctrine of grace, "the full and whole action of Christ in us"[31] and had no sympathy for the two leading Jansenists, Saint-Cyran (d. 1643) and Cornelius Jansen (d. 1638).

The followers of Molina, according to these extremists, were semi-pelagian, the humanists entirely so. Nothing but moral laxity could therefore be expected, and certainly a form of exaggerated humanism grew up in the seventeenth century which was bound to cause alarm. Above all though, the need to sanctify the intellect by means of active faith (as well as the appetitive powers by hope, charity and the subordinate moral virtues) was a practical necessity not yet recognized by the devotees of natural culture, and this gave the Jansenists their best opening for destructive criticism. Under the circumstances, even the liberal spirit of St. Francis of Sales was attacked. Saint-Cyran, Jansen and Arnauld (d. 1694) thus set themselves to the self-appointed task of spiritual and sacramental reform within the Church. Penance; solitude; death to the senses; total suppression of nature and exaggerated humility in approaching the sacraments; an end to all habits of familiarity with our Lady—such were the key characteristics of their cheerless outlook.

## 6 THE SEVENTEENTH-CENTURY IGNATIAN SCHOOL IN FRANCE

The French Ignatian school had begun to develop prior to Jansenism, but had its full flowering later.[32] Devotion to the Incarnate Word was particularly marked, also its rejection of exaggerated optimism as manifested by the humanists. In the main, however, it seems to have been preoccupied with the natural depravity of man in much the same way as de Bérulle himself, and its mystical teaching was restricted to the field of the subjective. If a man was heroic enough to attain moral perfection despite the corruption of the world at large, surely his sanctified will would suffice for all else. Antony Le Gaudier (d. 1622) was outstanding for his Christological writings, also John Baptist Saint-Jure (d. 1657). Julian Hayneuve (d. 1663) summed up their ideal saying: "If we would live according to truth, as we ought to live, Jesus must be our life. This means that he quickens our hearts and is the principle of all that we do, that our soul breathes only with him, that our mind thinks no other thoughts and our will has no other affections than those which come from him, that our body is never so bold as to move without his permission and at his discretion: in short, that the Incarnate Word governs us as absolutely as he governed his holy manhood."[33]

Louis Lallemant (d. 1635) is best known for his teaching on mysticism as presented by two of his disciples, John Rigoleuc and J. J. Surin, both of the Society of Jesus. His great devotion to the God-man was further characterized by a special love for our Lady and St. Joseph, also for the angels most closely associated with the Incarnation; but his emphasis on the interior guidance of the Holy Spirit was held in great suspicion by his superiors. On the face of it, Lallemant's assertions seem reasonable enough—these being to the effect that the Holy Spirit will sanctify the soul in proportion as the heart is cleansed or emptied of self and the will has been faithful in co-operating with the divine promptings—but his deeper purification of the intellect is restricted to the purely negative process of rejecting unwanted concepts and images by means of the will. He admitted all the basic means of strengthening the will, as recommended in the Exercises of St. Ignatius, and he appreciated theoretically the function of sanctifying grace in relation to all the infused virtues and gifts, but there is still no evidence that his mystical experience exceeded the ordinary flowering in wisdom of acquired contemplation. For all his habit of docility to the movements of the Holy Spirit, his experience was never passive in the sense required by St. Teresa in her last three mansions. In most ways, then, Lallemant's doctrine is comparable with that of the Jesuit mystics in Spain, also with the writings of the Carmelite theologians after the time of St. John of the Cross. It does not touch on the deeper meaning of infused contemplation.

John Joseph Surin (d. 1665) is the best known of Lallemant's disciples. As a boy he was influenced by Mother Isabel of the Angels, the Spanish nun who founded the Carmel in Bordeaux, but he decided at the age of sixteen to enter the Jesuit novitiate. As time went on, he began to suffer from nervous depression alternating with extreme elation, and for a long period he seems to have been subject to diabolical possession. His behaviour was a source of continual anxiety to his superiors, yet he was incapable of seeing himself in the wrong. One of his most powerful critics was the Calced Carmelite friar, John Chéron, who in 1657 published in Paris a book entitled *Examen de la Théologie Mystique*. The object of this book was to bring mysticism under the control of scholastic theology, re-establishing the function of reason in the interior life, together with the enlightenment provided by theological doctrine. In particular, he stressed the extent to which nature and the devil may simulate the divine action in the soul, should this control be neglected.

In Brittany, no less than in the Aquitanian Jesuit province, fear of mystical delusion became very strong during the second half of the seventeenth century. Francis Guilloré (d. 1684) therefore set out to instruct directors in the art of discernment, also to lay down practical rules for the guidance of individual souls. Like Cardinal de Bérulle, he had great devotion to the Sacred Humanity but always in terms of self-annihilation, abjection, poverty and abandonment. He looked upon the Heart of Jesus as a symbol of our Lord's inner life, and would have us believe that this Heart was perpetually engulfed in grief and sorrow. Vincent Huby, on the other hand (d. 1693), preached and wrote incessantly about divine love, death to self, and devotion to the Sacred Heart. Missionary work spread, and many retreat-houses were founded in Normandy and Paris as well as in Brittany.

## 7   THE RISE AND FALL OF QUIETISM

Quietism, like most heresies, aimed at the misrepresentation or distortion of true doctrine, in order that the good eventually to be achieved by that doctrine might at least be hindered in its development. Thus the *particular* good, which quietism aimed at rendering obscure, is the true nature of substantial mystical union as taught by St. John of the Cross, also by St. Teresa of Avila during the last years of her life, and every error expressed is like a "spoiled negative" of the truth ultimately to be revealed.

Now Jansenism, on the pretext of making the people more worthy of the sacraments, had aimed only at their ultimate estrangement from God's merciful love; insidiously it had sown the seeds of paralysing fear and even of despair where fallen nature is concerned, for no man can hope to be perfected except

10

first he be nourished by the Bread of Life. Quietism, then, was to complete this destructive programme by inculcating a presumptive hope in the operations of divine love, at the expense of living faith and of all the norms of Christian prudence. The so-called "pure faith" of the quietist means *total inertia* of the intellect, his "pure hope" a form of *indifference* to everything, even to salvation, and his "pure love" a state of *abandonment* to whatever impulse happened to assail his will. This new heresy did not reach its peak until the end of the seventeenth century, but its seeds were being sown in France, Spain and Italy many years before that; so too did its doctrines continue to appear in modified forms long after the Holy See had condemned the writings of Michael Molinos and Madame de Guyon, together with the maxims of Fénelon. The forerunners of the movement have been called "pre-quietists",[34] the more modern exponents of the doctrine "semi-quietists".[35]

Before quietism can gain its foothold in the human soul, the ground has to be prepared for it. Quietism cannot attack sanctifying grace *directly*, nor—as in Jansenism—does it aim primarily at withdrawing the soul from the sacraments. Rather is it concerned with a gradual destruction of the *spirit of faith*, which would otherwise be empowering the soul to profit from the sacraments to the full. This destruction can be achieved by varying techniques, but always with the same spirit of pride and independence at their root, leading in turn to mental laziness, indifference to the Sacred Humanity, and lack of consistency in the practice of virtue. Alleged mystical experiences of a subjective character, often accompanied by great fire and sweetness, foster the illusion of sanctity still further—whilst all the time the hidden rift between the will and right reason continues to deepen, and self-criticism is rendered impossible. Quietist doctrine is powerless to harm souls who are properly grounded in the teaching of the Church, who devote themselves to the Sacred Humanity of our Lord, and who practise interior obedience to their lawful superiors as well as exterior conformity; but, in the absence of these safeguards, its action is as swift as that of a match applied to dry brushwood. Let us then examine in greater detail how the soul's defences may come to be undermined, either by the devil or by our own foolishness.

*Quietism and the Intelligence:* If one wants to prevent a person from acting in a certain way, one has either to render that action impossible, or else to convince the person that the action will not achieve the purpose intended, even supposing that he does perform it. Again it may be suggested that the precise opposite will result, if the person is foolish enough to take the risk. Now in genuinely mystical prayer, the normal activity of the mind may be impeded by God in two ways: either through the involuntary *suspension* of the exterior and interior senses as in the ecstatic or near-ecstatic states; or through the *ligature* of the powers, produced by the intensity of infused faith and giving the impression of interior darkness. But in quietism, on the other hand, efforts are made to produce this negative state through sheer will-power and even to suppress such acts of prayer as may present themselves to the conscious mind. More subtle still, the soul is taught to regard the activity of the mind— even if unavoidable—as useless. Mystics of the strongly affective type have always mistrusted the activity of the mind at the best of times, since for them it has seemed a poor instrument by comparison with the heart, but this in itself does not amount to culpable error. Error here involves the *deliberate, calculated suppression* of the activity of a God-given power which he himself has intended us to use for our greater perfection. Those who write and preach incessantly about divine love, to the exclusion of all else, are often the unwitting promotors of intellectual laziness in those who ought to be treading a different interior path altogether, but usually their doctrine is not harmful in itself

unless seized upon by those of evil intent and used in illustration
of something quite different. Any doctrine of a "simplified"
nature—for example, the *Rule of Perfection* by Benet of Canfield,
the Italian translation of which was condemned by the Holy
Office in 1689—exposes itself to this kind of misinterpretation.
Thus Benet of Canfield (d. 1611) sought to reduce everything
to the practice of fervent good will in union with God; John de
Bernières, an influential layman (d. 1659) whose writings were
condemned in 1689 and 1690, exaggerated the rôle of humiliation,
self-abandonment, and spiritual indifference in the interior life;
and even the famous archdeacon, Henry Boudon (d. 1702),
wrote so fervently but ambiguously about holy love, that the
quietists made full use of his book *Dieu Seul*, causing it to be
placed on the Index in 1688.

*Quietism and the Will:* By the year 1670, Pourrat tells us,
"the prayer of simple regard was practised almost everywhere
in France"[36]—a statement fully endorsed by the Jesuit, Francis
Guilloré, Here, it seemed, was the ideal short-cut to intimate
union with God: no effort was required, just a facility for making
God a projection of self and for resting in the concept formed.
In the absence of a director and of opportunities for practising
supernatural virtue, self-deception could hardly be avoided; but
had not Cardinal de Bérulle laid down that "submission of self
to God" was the one thing necessary, as distinct from possessing
"a high insight into the attributes of the divinity . . . which few
have"?[37] The argument was indeed a subtle one! Nonetheless,
the genuine prayer of simple regard is the equivalent of that
prayer of simplicity or acquired contemplation taught by the
Spanish Carmelite school, but only as applied to those whose
minds have already been developed to the full by means of
meditation, affective considerations, spiritual reading and objective study of the theological principles laid down by the Church.
Apart from the Teresian methods of active recollection in union

with the Sacred Humanity, anything else is merely pious reverie, and even J. J. Surin defined false mystics as those who, "though God does not call them to this state, read those who write about it, or talk with those who talk about it, endlessly".[38] The less virtue a soul possesses, the more spiritually ambitious it is liable to become, and no one knows this better than the devil himself.

*Quietism and the Sacred Humanity:* As early as 1605, Mother Anne of Jesus—who brought a party of St. Teresa's nuns, first to Paris, then to the Low Countries—had written to a Spanish bishop remarking on the absence of devotion to the Sacred Humanity and saying that the French seemed to think of nothing but union with God by means of suspension of the faculties. The Jesuits and the Berullian school, as we have seen, contributed greatly to the new Sacred Heart devotion, but their determination to spiritualize our Lord led inevitably to a practical disregard for his manhood. Before long, then, both this manhood and all the other mysteries of our Lord's life on earth were formally excluded from the contemplation of the quietists. As for Madame Guyon, she cherished everything concerning "passive prayer" and "naked faith", and later made use of this terminology to illustrate her own exaggerated doctrines.

*Quietism and the Moral Virtues:* The impact of quietism on the moral virtues in general and on chastity in particular was not immediately apparent. Quietism does not begin its operations in the sensitive field, because it would then be recognized too quickly, and no one of good will would approve of an evil that had been condemned already by the law of God. In seventeenth-century France, above all, the technique had to be one of teaching people *to ignore* the human body, then *to raise themselves* to great spiritual heights, finally *to assume* that their flesh was no longer able to impinge itself on their lofty sanctity. Grave unchastity in those who profess to be perfect is always preceded by spiritual or intellectual pride. In France, as is well known, the moral crisis came to a head in the persons of Madame Guyon and Fr. La Combe, in Spain and Italy in the persons of Michael Molinos and his followers. Molinos even went so far as to say that "God allows and wills the devil to violate the bodies of some perfect souls and make them do wicked things, with all their wits about them and without feeling any scruple".[39] The emotionalism of Fr. La Combe and the epileptic hysteria of Madame Guyon add nothing to this doctrinal picture. In every variation, "leave God to act" is the recurring theme.

The condemnation of quietist errors in France, including the teaching of Madame Guyon, was completed in March 1695 after nearly eight months of discussion at Issy between Bossuet, the Bishop of Châlons, and M. Tronson (the superior at Saint-Sulpice). Fénelon, who had meantime been consecrated Archbishop of Cambrai, continued to disagree in private with Bossuet on the subject of disinterested love, passive prayer and certain mystical trials; and this led to the modification of several of the articles drawn up, also to the publication of Fénelon's *Maxims of the Saints*, which were condemned by the Holy See in 1700 on account of their exaggerated teaching about pure love and its professed indifference concerning reward or punishment.

Apart from the errors condemned by the Church, there were several other points of difference between Bossuet and Fénelon, concerning which no pronouncement was made. These concerned such matters as the nature of charity, the nature of passive prayer, and the nature of passive contemplation.[40] In these disputes, neither side contributed to more than part of the truth; but in matters of spiritual direction, Bossuet was always more objective than Fénelon, preferring theological principle before all else in the task of establishing the reign of divine love in the soul. Fénelon was no less concerned with the amendment of the soul by means of divine love, but for him the affective approach was the means to be adopted. Thus the difference between the two archbishops was largely a matter of individual temperament.

The general effect on mysticism of the quietist crisis was both paralysing and disastrous, especially as it led to a revival of Jansenism and the invasion of moral theology by a similar rigorism. Orthodox spirituality became increasingly aggressive and suspicious of novelty, and this unhappy atmosphere continued to prevail throughout the eighteenth century, even during the first half of the nineteenth century. It is true that great steps were taken in the field of education—by St. John Baptist de la Salle, for example, and St. Louis Grignion de Montfort—but this alone would not have sufficed to check the general cooling of theological virtue in the hearts of the faithful, let alone to offset the growing distrust concerning devotion to the Sacred Heart of Jesus. None but God could heal the wounds which man in his blind zeal had inflicted upon the Church. With the raising up of St. Alphonsus Liguori in Italy, then, a new age of hope began to dawn.

[1] *Spiritual Canticle*, XL; p. 212, Vol. 2, L. G. & Co.
[2] Pourrat, Vol. 3, p. 227.
[3] *De Oratione*, lib. II, cap. xii, 2; quoted by Pourrat, p. 225.
[4] See Op. cit., lib. II, cap. xvi.
[5] Thor-Salviat, A. A, *Secrets of a Seraph*, trans. Pausback, p. 117.
[6] Op. cit., p. 172.
[7] Pourrat, Vol. 3, p. 233.
[8] *Souvenirs et Avis*, Vol. 1, p. 413; quoted by Pourrat, p. 271.
[9] *Devout Life*, Part One, Ch. 3; quoted by Pourrat, p. 281.
[10] See *S.T.*, II–II, q. 82, art. 1.
[11] *Love of God*, Bk. 1, Ch, 12; quoted by Pourrat, p. 311.
[12] Loc. cit.
[13] *Deposition*, Art. xxiv; quoted by Pourrat, p. 312.
[14] *Oeuvres Complètes*, p. 880; quoted by Pourrat, p. 329.
[15] Op. cit., p. 879; quoted by Pourrat, p. 329.
[16] *Grandeurs de Jèsus*, Discourse II; quoted by Pourrat, p. 332.
[17] Op. cit., Discourses II–IV; quoted by Pourrat, pp. 333–4.
[18] See Houssaye, Vol. III, p. 493; referred to by Pourrat, p. 334.
[19] See Pourrat, Vol. 3, pp. 335–45.

[20]*Grandeurs de Jésus*, Discourse II; quoted by Pourrat, p. 336.

[21]*Oeuvres Complètes*, p. 1179; quoted by Pourrat, p. 349.

[22]*Catéchisme Chrétien*, Part One, lesson xx; quoted by Pourrat, p. 361.

[23]*L'Idée du Sacerdoce et du sacrifice de Jésus-Christ*, p. 60; quoted by Pourrat, p. 351.

[24]Cf. Vonier, *Sketches and Studies in Theology*, pp. 77–8.

[25]Pourrat, Vol. 3, p. 382.

[26]*Coeur Admirable*, Bk. I, Ch. 2; quoted by Pourrat, p. 399.

[27]Cf. Lebrun on St. John Eudes; quoted by Pourrat, p. 400.

[28]Pourrat, Vol. 4, p. 1.

[29]Pourrat, Vol. 4, pp. 3–30.

[30]Opuscula, p. 7; quoted by Pourrat, Vol. 4, p. 5.

[31]Pourrat, Vol. 4, pp. 8–9.

[32]See Pourrat, Vol. 4, pp. 39–61.

[33]*Meditations;* quoted by Pourrat, Vol. 4, p. 45.

[34]See Pourrat, Vol. 4, Chs. 5–7.

[35]See Farges, *Mystical Phenomena*, pp. 139–47.

[36]Pourrat, Vol. 4, p. 123.

[37] See p. 136.

[38]*Dialogues Spirituels*, p. 112; quoted by Pourrat, p. 132.

[39]Molinos, Prop. 41; quoted by Pourrat, p. 167.

[40]Pourrat, Vol. 4, pp. 227–32.

## PART FIVE

# THEOLOGICAL HOPE UNDER TRIAL

## FOREWORD

AFTER THE Council of Trent (1545–63), during the immediate post-Reformation era in particular, the faith of the Church was necessarily the subject of special attention, and we have seen in the fourth part of this study how circumstances combined to maintain the emphasis on fundamental doctrine for so long. As the late Abbot Vonier, O.S.B., has remarked: "In ancient Christian language the terms faith and Church are synonymous: you belong to the Church because you share her great faith. This is the triumphant achievement of the Spirit, of the God of truth, whose operations are supreme and irresistible: he maintains here on earth that wonderful thing—faith, and this he achieves independently of man's moral worth and sanctity";[1] again: "Those theologians are right who consider faith to be the Church's body, her flesh and bone; so that faith may be called the substance of the Church, her constitution, her stature."[2]

It is clear, then, that the faith of the Church can never be destroyed or diminished by the trials to which it is subjected; but what we may term the "fruitfulness" of faith involves the perfection of the other two theological virtues as well—most immediately of all, the quality of man's hope. Faith sets about building in accordance with the divine plans, quickened in its activity by the free gift of grace which gave it birth in the Heart of Christ; but man is still free to prefer the attractions set in his path by the world and the flesh, and the devil loses no opportunity in promoting the deception of the human heart on precisely these lines. Greater material prosperity, for example, has long been the boast of the reformed churches in seeking to win the allegiance of the Catholic poor, above all for the purpose of establishing state-control in Catholic countries. Bigger and better trades and industries, better schools, hospitals and welfare services, protective insurances and pensions, even the alleged right to limit the population by sinful means and to exterminate those who are a burden to society, all these material bribes are set in the path of God's children for the purpose of leading them astray, and all too often they succeed, temporarily at least. We have remarked on the outstanding social achievements of the Church from the sixteenth century onwards, above all in the establishment of hospitals and schools run on voluntary lines, but as Vonier points out in his essay on "The Catholic Church and Progress", Catholicism "had not in the past to deal with an innumerable population without property". Social science today "is chiefly concerned with that section of mankind which has been created by the industrial age".[3] This challenge has been met by the magnificent directives of Leo XIII and Pius XI in their social encyclical letters;[4] but again it has been one of the tests of theological hope to put this teaching into practice, especially in countries where Catholics are still in the minority and where income is already taxed heavily to pay for the state-departments. Under the circumstances, it is small wonder that science should have presented itself as the new god to be worshipped: the antithesis of the superstitious ignorance attributed to the Catholic Church by her enemies.

Now the spirituality of the seventeenth and eighteenth centuries, as we have seen, was predominantly active, being threatened on the one hand by the false idealism of the Jansenists and undermined on the other hand by the subtlety of the quietists, but virile nonetheless, especially in France and Italy, and renewing its fundamentals as though the catastrophe of the Protestant Reformation had never happened. The study and contemplation of the great doctrinal truths, especially those concerned with the mystery of the Incarnation and the divine attributes as revealed by the God-man, characterized all the leading theologians and churchmen of the day; yet it is significant that their vision did not exceed the limits of the spiritual contemplation of St. John of the Cross. In many cases, certainly, there was abundant evidence of a connatural participation or enjoyment by the will of the interior light of faith received; but beneath it all, there remained the Augustinian pessimism about the weakness of the flesh which the Berullian school had magnified still further, and because of this—also on account of its influence on eucharistic theology—the work of theological hope in transforming the memory was seriously impeded. In the same way, by reason of this psychological impediment to perfect interior development free from all strain, the secrets of the last three mansions of St. Teresa remained a closed book.

With the further catastrophe of the French Revolution in 1789, all the religious orders in France were driven out of the country for nearly half a century; so hope, divested of all else, sought expression in the relief of the destitute, in educational work among the poor, and in the possibilities of missionary endeavour. John Joseph Allemand (1772–1836), for example, was ordained in secret at the height of the Terror and devoted himself to the welfare of the young people in France with a zeal similar to that of St. John Bosco in Italy; St. John Baptist Vianney (1785–1859) won back thousands of souls each year through his own heroic confidence in the sacrament of penance; no less than seven women foundresses gave themselves to the education of girls; the Little Sisters of the Poor were founded in 1840, the year of the Dominican restoration in Paris and three years after the Benedictine restoration at Solesmes, followed in

1865 by the Little Sisters of the Assumption; and Ven. Antony Chevrier (1826–79) spent his whole priestly life teaching religion to neglected children in Lyons. For the proper understanding of nineteenth-century spirituality and its subsequent developments, it is necessary then to examine some of these points more closely, also to go back a little in order to appreciate the co-ordinating rôle of St. Alphonsus Liguori, not only in regard to moral theology, but also in the sphere of mystical theology and of devotion to the *Mother of Holy Hope*, our blessed Lady.

## I   ST. ALPHONSUS LIGUORI: MARTYR OF PATIENCE

The spiritual achievements of St. Alphonsus Liguori could hardly have been more prodigious, nor yet more far-reaching in the life of the Church. Small in stature, unassuming in appearance, he in every way exemplified the Augustinian saying that power not size is the cause of greatness. Born in 1696, the eldest of seven children, his father planned that he should excel as an advocate and educated him accordingly, with special attention to the liberal arts and to social accomplishments as well. At the early age of sixteen, he qualified as a Doctor of Laws in the University of Naples and embarked immediately on a brilliant career at the bar. One day, however, providence permitted that he should make a fool of himself through a serious misinterpretation of evidence; and from that moment on, life for Alphonsus was never the same. The incident haunted him. His self-sufficiency was shattered. With his father's ultimate consent, therefore, he trained as a secular missionary priest and was ordained at the age of thirty.

The new career of the future saint thus found expression initially in the slums of Naples amidst the sick, the poor, and the beggars whom he organized as a confraternity. The deeper purpose of all this must certainly have been hidden at the time. When a man's natural kingdom has crumbled to dust, he not infrequently seeks to console those who are worse off than himself, and out of this very abasement his new dignity grows up. Alphonsus himself had wished to join the Oratorians, but his father would not allow it. Today we recognize him as one of the greatest champions of the poor and illiterate that the Church has ever known, not only in the matter of material benefits, but above all as regards their spiritual perfection. More than a hundred years before, St. Francis of Sales had astonished society by teaching the ways of interior perfection to men and women of education living in the world, whereas before such practices were regarded as suitable for priests and religious only; but now, just at the time when Jansenism had renewed its stranglehold over the consciences of the people and quietism was reaping its harvest of delusion and immorality, the treasures of the Kingdom were being offered—pressed down and shaken together and running over—to the Neapolitan down-and-outs, a perfect example of the folly of the Cross. Grace according to St. Alphonsus is always sufficient and inclusive of the power to pray, but it only becomes efficacious *if a man does pray*. Therefore it is a matter of primary importance to teach every man to pray, not merely the well-educated or those with time on their hands. The Passion of our Lord is a book from which all may read, and St. Alphonsus—although he urged the practice of visits to the Blessed Sacrament and of devoting a regular period in the early morning to mental prayer—always insisted that there was no form of occupation wherein a man could not raise his mind and heart to God. God would assist him in this matter. Despite his own brilliance of intellect, the whole trend of the teaching of St. Alphonsus on prayer is affective, and always with the special object of the prayer of petition uppermost, namely the grace of a good death and eternal salvation. As he was later to declare at the beginning of his *Practice of the Love of Jesus Christ:* "The whole sanctity and perfection of a soul consists in loving Jesus Christ, our God, our sovereign good, and our Redeemer".[5] He did not begin writing for publication until nearly 1745, the fiftieth year of his life, but after that fame came quickly, thanks to the support of Pope Benedict XIV over the printing of his *Moral Theology* first issued in 1748.

While training for the priesthood, St. Alphonsus had been formed by a certain canon of the rigorist school, and the constant emphasis on the divine justice at the expense of God's merciful fatherhood was in deep contrast with his own compassionate heart and preoccupation with the goodness of God. After ordination, however, he continued to follow the principles which had been instilled into him—preaching a salutary fear where necessary, and not always absolving his penitents immediately— yet without harshness, and always with the thought of the divine mercy uppermost. After founding the Congregation of the Most Holy Redeemer, he resolved to teach theology himself, by which time his practical experience in the pastoral field was sufficient to add weight to his earlier convictions, and it is here that we benefit to the full from the marriage between his legal training and his missionary labours in the Neapolitan slums. As Pope Pius IX declared when proclaiming him a Doctor of the Church in 1871, this new moral system was the decisive blow in the uprooting of Jansenism, and his subsequent devotional works completed the process.

The Congregation of the Most Holy Redeemer originated in a manner no less unexpected than any other aspect of the saint's career. A nun sought his help in obtaining episcopal sanction for the new congregation which she desired to form, and his recommendation in this matter was so effective that the support of the local bishop was promptly secured. This same nun, Sr. Maria Celeste, then predicted the foundation of a community of men-religious, and seems to have exercised considerable influence over St. Alphonsus in this respect. At all events, the first community of Redemptorists was formed the following year—1732—with the Bishop of Castellamare as superior. As might be expected, this arrangement led to every kind of disagreement and divergence of opinion concerning the work to be undertaken, also to the withdrawal of all but two of the original community, and it was not until six years after the death of the saint in 1787 that the original Redemptorist Rule was given state-recognition in Naples, thus leading to the restoration of the congregation. St. Alphonsus was beatified in 1816, canonized in 1839, and thirty-two years later declared a Doctor of the Church. So marvellously did his life personify the trials through which the Church herself had to pass in the nineteenth century, that we would do well to examine more closely both the events which took place after his sixty-sixth year and the effect of these on his writings. The words of St. Gregory which he quotes in *The Practice of the Love of Jesus Christ* sum up all: "We can be martyrs without the sword if we keep patience."[6]

In 1747 at the age of fifty-one, fifteen years after the foundation of his congregation, St. Alphonsus had been urged by the King of Naples to become Archbishop of Palermo. He had refused this honour, but in 1762 the Pope required him to accept the see of Sant' Agata de' Goti, a town near Naples. There amidst a flock largely illiterate he laboured for nearly thirteen years, ever giving priority to the reform of the clergy, also to the spiritual and corporal works of mercy as he did in the early days of his priesthood. "If we would give full satisfaction to the heart of God," he said, in his treatise on *Conformity to the Divine Will*, "we must bring our own will in everything into conformity with his, and . . . into uniformity too . . . This is the sum and substance of that perfection to which we ought ever to aspire; this is what must be the aim of all our works, and of all our desires, meditations and prayers."[7] It is however by faith and prayer only that such constancy can be achieved, and so it follows that the virtue of hope has a central rôle in every interior operation. "By prayer we can do all things," he says, "for by this means God will give us that strength which we need."[8] Some have praised the ease with which St. Alphonsus introduced the teaching of the saints and doctors into his own instructions, but there is no doubt whatever that the power of these writings to stir the mind and heart of others was born of his own heroic virtue during those long years when everything and everyone seemed to be failing him or acting against him. Most striking of all, too, was his unfailing devotion to our blessed Lady, the Mother of Holy Hope, and this in an age when the clergy were so apprehensive about the Jansenistic criticism of all Mariological works. Openly and fearlessly he taught that every grace coming to us from God is bestowed upon us through Mary, and he shows by means of simple reasoning in his treatise *The Glories of Mary* why it is that God wishes us to place in her all our hopes of salvation and every blessing, why it is that "to supplicate the Virgin with such hope is not to distrust the mercy of God, but only to fear our own unworthiness".[9] So clear, so resolute, so immovable was St. Alphonsus in these convictions, that Jansenism melted before them like ice in the spring sunshine.

From 1768 onwards, St. Alphonsus had suffered first from rheumatic fever then from a crippling form of arthritis, and in 1775 Pope Pius VI allowed him to retire from his episcopal see to one of the nine Redemptorist houses now in existence. Four years later came permission to establish the congregation canonically with a novitiate house and house of studies, to which end the rule was revised and taken out of the founder's hands entirely. Bewilderment ensued, so Pius VI intervened personally, transplanted the congregation to the papal states under direct obedience to himself, and finally expelled St. Alphonsus from his community as the alleged cause of the trouble. The humiliation of the octogenarian founder was complete, neither did he live to see the end of his disgrace. Physical, mental and spiritual anguish engulfed him on every side, reminding one particularly of the last eighteen months of the life of St. Thérèse of Lisieux more than a hundred years later, but still at the end of it all he was perfectly resigned to God's holy will, perfectly confident that our Lady would not betray his filial trust in her Immaculate Heart. During the last two years of his life, he experienced a great interior calm, then died not long before his ninety-first birthday. Pius VI, the same pope who had persecuted him so bitterly, declared him venerable in 1798.

The teaching of St. Alphonsus on mental prayer is a close reflexion of all that passed during the sixty years and more of his priesthood. He did not add anything new to the science of mystical theology, beyond distinguishing the essential from the extraordinary in the life of St. Teresa, but he rendered this science a very great service by summarizing the ascetical and mystical doctrine of St. Teresa in an appendix to his *Praxis confessarii*.[10] The nature of his own mystical experience can perhaps be deduced from the nature of his sufferings, but there is no doubt that he had a better understanding of the affective degrees of Teresian mystical union than of the substantial experience. In short, for all that St. Alphonsus refers to the nights of sense and spirit and the virtues to be practised therein, he is more familiar with the St. Teresa of the *Life* and the *Way of Perfection* than with the St. Teresa of the *Interior Castle*, and this in fact is the case with most of the Teresian commentators. Humility, obedience, and the absolute committal of self to the Mother of Divine Mercy, these are the virtues which he stresses most for souls in the obscure night;[11] but whenever the sweet attraction of infused contemplation is experienced, the soul should not interrupt this union of loving attention by trying to reason or

11

make further acts.[12] The love and respect which St. Alphonsus had for St. Teresa is well known, also he frequently quoted St. John of the Cross in his devotional writings; so the Carmelite order in turn should thank God for the interest and protection of this great doctor of the Church, the champion of the saints, the lifelong upholder of devotion to our Lady and St. Joseph. The true friends of God are ever ready to assist one another in all their undertakings for the greater glory of the Church.

## 2   THE AFTERMATH OF QUIETISM

"Pray, pray, never cease to pray; for if you pray, your salvation will be secure, but if you stop praying your damnation will be certain"[13]—thus did St. Alphonsus Liguori conclude his short treatise on prayer, and there is no theme in any of his writings which recurs more frequently or with greater emphasis. Confidence in God, confidence in our Lady, but always a distrust of self and of one's own strength: such was his message for us, and if pious souls in the following centuries had been guided by the vigorous spirituality of the Liguorian school, the hidden presumption of semi-quietism would never have acquired such disturbing proportions.

The first, though not in practice the most dangerous, aspect of semi-quietism which we must note, is its professed disinterestedness in salvation. Hope, it was claimed, must concern itself with the glory of God only, since otherwise it will be tainted with self; hope must be indifferent to every consideration of personal happiness or reward. This erroneous view, which was a favourite one in the mind of Fénelon, seems in retrospect to have been the outcome of muddled thinking rather than of deliberate theological misrepresentation. The glory of God and his desire for each one of us to choose the way of salvation is in fact *indivisible*, and the actual benefit to fallen man is no more than secondary to the more fundamental aspect of the Incarnation. As Scheeben so well expresses it:—

> The glory of God and of Christ himself is the highest aim, and the love of God for himself and for Christ is the highest motive of the Incarnation. Often as the holy Fathers assign the necessary restoration of fallen man as the end of the Incarnation, and God's mercy as its motive, no less often do they insist that God in his overflowing love has decreed to give us incalculably more, and to elevate us incomparably higher after the Incarnation than he had done before. [14]

It is true, as we have seen, that souls may reach a degree of union with our Lord where they cease to be preoccupied with speculation about the future life, and—under the influence of his personal direction—devote themselves wholly to the needs of the Church upon earth; but this "gift" of supernatural indifference is prepared for by the exercise of faith in the intellect and the concurrence of hope in the memory, *not* by acts of the will which can only lead to strain and self-deception. As Mgr. Guerry says, the kind of bitter warfare which is otherwise waged against self by devout souls, is indeed "the cause of much spiritual ineffectiveness . . . In the spiritual life, as in all human activities, God wishes that the intelligence should come first, and that it should be guided by the light of reason, of faith, and of the gifts of the Holy Ghost". [15]

The basic reason, it seems, why so many souls since the end of the seventeenth century have lost their interior balance over the practice of "holy abandonment" concerns the haste with which they have tried to lose themselves in the prayer of simple regard. We have already remarked on the difference between this and acquired contemplation as practised in Spain, but it will be helpful if we now examine this point in greater detail. Interior simplification, in fact, can be the outcome of three distinct processes: the exercise of the intellect in faith, the exercise of the heart in love, and the devotion of the will through the consistent practice of supernatural virtue in union with Jesus and Mary. Each process, moreover, has its own particular psychology.[16]

The deliberate and consistent exercise of faith in the intellect normally presupposes the practice of all the other supernatural virtues too, and of this is born the Catholic scholar and theologian, even in some cases the Catholic genius. Allied or co-ordinated with strongly developed affective powers as well, the likely outcome will be a saint or doctor of the Church, but only where there are no flaws in the spiritual armour caused by pride in its various forms. Psychological defects, on the other hand— such as the pessimism of St. Augustine about original sin, and the natural fear of concupiscence which has handicapped so many spirits otherwise born for greatness—do not necessarily impede sanctity. They may prevent the soul in this life from attaining to the fruition of the last three mansions of St. Teresa, but at least they encourage the basic dispositions required for this interior flowering, namely a deep humility, detachment from creatures for their own sake, and dependence on actual grace. A true saint, as St. Alphonsus Liguori has said, resembles "the sun, ever uniform in his serenity under whatever circumstances may come to pass, because his contentment lies in his uniformity to the divine will".[17]

The intensification of affective prayer (when no longer the direct outcome of discursive faith) provides far greater scope for self-deception, and it must always be distrusted if a corresponding delicacy of conscience and fidelity to duties of state are not discernible. Further, since there is no fixed level of intellectual development for the individual soul, what matters is that each must attain to its own maximum. In practice, however, the tendency is for the soul to be satisfied, and even to rejoice in its supposed achievement in relation to lesser minds, therefore to stop short in its search for truth, to relax the effort in so far as fresh pioneering activity is concerned, and to pursue the sensible delights of divine love instead. In the case of men, this results—at best—in a form of Christian humanism; in the case of women (apart from those who devote themselves with success to the masculine professions) to a state of mind wherein emotional fervour and aridity alternate, and the strain on the essential will-to-perfection can become very intense. Women, it is true, whether living in the cloister or the world, ordinarily have far less opportunity for going deeply into things, since even if the necessary leisure can be secured there is still the problem of physical or nervous fatigue to be reckoned with, and therefore they tend to rely on strength of feeling for compensation; yet the fact remains that no day's work is more exhausting than emotional frustration, no spiritual tonic more invigorating than the discovery of fresh intellectual horizons, and that is why Mgr. Guerry makes the "light of faith" *a first necessity* in the attainment of self-oblivion. By means of this light, he says, "the soul discovers the grandeur, the perfection, the rights of Christ; the transcendence of God, and the littleness and misery of man. This light shines forth and shows the way that is to be followed. The life of Jesus can grow within us, only if the self does not usurp us entirely."[18] For the practice of supernatural virtue unaided by this inspiration from the mind, there is no doubting the heroism required; yet to act in this way is no less absurd than to go through life blindfolded, neither does any special merit attach to it. The more we intensify our spirit of faith, the greater are our chances of being delivered from the aridities of the third mansion and the bewildering helplessness of the night of sense.

The French semi-quietists after the time of Fénelon did not go so far as to ignore our Lord entirely (although devotion to his Sacred Humanity has always been regarded as an exercise for beginners only), but by dint of concentrating on the practice of charity *without* the supporting enlightenment of faith and the steadying effect of positive hope, their concept of him gradually became exposed to subjective error, even as in the case of well-meaning Protestants. Love that is born of the consideration of *objective truth* is a very different quality to the affectivity that can be stirred up through appealing to the senses and emotions, and if this latter affectivity is relied upon as a proximate means of contemplative union, there is certainly nothing surprising about the subsequent aridity. Affective writings to be of use in the practical sphere, must at least enlighten and encourage the soul in the exercise of virtue; otherwise they are food merely for love of self. Again, while it is true that prayer consists in much loving rather than in much thinking, we still have to distinguish between surface feelings and that deep conviction which alone can feed our essential devotedness in the service of God. To this end, then, we need *light*—the light that comes to us from the positive knowledge of Jesus Christ in all his mysteries, and this against a background of self-disillusionment supernaturally effected. Self-examination in the light of reason is the work of the Pharisee.

By the end of the nineteenth century—at the level of theological discussion—three possible views of mysticism evolved out of the fire of controversy and led to still further intellectual battles. First, there was the conservative view which looked upon mysticism as the experience of deeply affective souls only, therefore as having the degrees of "suspension" as its measure. Ascetical practice, first in the purgative way then in accordance with interior illumination, was held to be the normal means of attaining to this union of intense love, a union exemplified by the famous ecstatics such as St. Bernard, St. Francis of Assisi and St. Mary Magdalen de' Pazzi. In the life of St. Teresa, on the other hand, we have seen how her teaching about affective prayer represented only one aspect of her mystical doctrine, and that she herself judged the substantial experience to be more important. Secondly, and in close relationship with the first view, was the opinion of writers like Canon Saudreau and Ludovic de Besse who not only regarded affective mysticism as the highest goal attainable, but further insisted on its being the necessary concomitant of interior perfection. They claimed that there was only *one way* for all, and that if the soul does not attain to these affective states, it has only itself to blame. Against this, Pope Benedict XIV—in laying down the rules for the beatification and canonization of saints—made *heroic virtue* the criterion of perfection, and practical experience has long disproved the necessity of subjective consolations for the attainment of this end. "True devotion and spirituality," says St. John of the Cross, "consist in perseverance in prayer, with patience and humility, distrusting yourself that you may please God only."[19] According to the third view, a dividing line had to be drawn between "high" or "strong" mystical states and those which are "weak" or "low". Only the chosen few were considered eligible for the former category, but everyone might aspire to the lower experience, which was inclusive of acquired contemplation and the prayer of quiet.[20] This last classification has inevitably caused bewilderment, since no one experienced in the matter would ever describe the soul in St. Teresa's last three mansions as being in a "high" or "strong" state, still less the contemplation of the fourth mansion as "weak" or "low". Acquired contemplation, moreover, was always associated with strength in the original meaning of the term. To understand these modern views, therefore, one has always to remember that most writers think of mysticism in terms of intense affectivity. Further, one must recall the extent to which the term "acquired contemplation" has been emasculated since the seventeenth century.

After the appearance in 1901 of *Graces of Interior Prayer* by

Auguste Poulain, S.J., mystical controversy became intensely heated and was still at its height in 1923, when—after the Discalced Carmelite Congress in Madrid—Mgr. Albert Farges brought out the second edition of his book entitled *Mystical Phenomena*. Many of the disputes were strictly terminological and might not have arisen if the theologians concerned had been accustomed to think of the mystical life in relation to the personal Christ. In recent years, a great advance in this respect has been made by Jean Mouroux in his book, *Je Crois en Toi, structure personelle de la foi*.[21] When examining the life of St. Thérèse of Lisieux, we may perhaps see more clearly what is really essential to mystical union with the Incarnate Word, as distinct from the subjective differences which tend to create such confusion in the minds of those who seek objective truth.

## 3   THE MODERN LITURGICAL REVIVAL

The French prayer of simple regard inevitably undermined the interest of the people in liturgical functions, since these derive their inner meaning from the mysteries of the Incarnation and Redemption, and no one can appreciate their practical importance—least of all in terms of everyday life—without a deep consideration of the supernatural truths involved. Certainly the value of private prayer and individual petition must not be underestimated, but always it is the corporate worship of the Church which ensures the deepest bonds of faith, hope and charity between the members of Christ's mystical body. Vonier therefore says that "the liturgical movement is, above all things, a renovation among us of the art of celebrating Christian feasts and consequently of presenting to the people the mysteries of God in a splendid fashion".[22]

In France, the liturgical revival really dates from the Benedictine Restoration at Solesmes in 1837, followed in 1840 by the publication of Abbot Guéranger's *Institutions Liturgiques*. For the encouragement of the spirit of prayer amongst the faithful, the abbot then produced a book known in English as *The Liturgical Year*. Such steps led to conflict with the upholders of devotional booklets and other forms of homely piety, but it did much to redress the balance between grandeur and silliness in matters of worship, and a hundred years later Pope Pius XII made it clear in his encyclical *Mystici Corporis* that "although public prayer, as proceeding from Mother Church herself, excels beyond any other by reason of the dignity of the Bride of Christ, nevertheless all prayers, even those said in the most private way, have their dignity and their efficacy, and are also of great value to the whole mystical body".[23] Again, in *Mediator Dei*, the forms of private devotion which Pius XII advocated particularly are: "meditation, examination of conscience, retreats, visits to the Blessed Sacrament, and special devotions to the blessed Virgin Mary, above all, of course, the Rosary".[24] "These devotional exercises," he continues, "cannot but be inspired and influenced by the Holy Ghost; in their various ways they tend to raise up the soul to God, to purify it from sin and urge it to the pursuit of virtue, and to give it a love for true piety; they accustom us to meditating upon the eternal truths and dispose us to contemplate the mysteries of the divinity and humanity of Christ. Moreover, nourishing the spiritual life of Christians as they do, they cause them to take part with greater profit in the public functions, and prevent the liturgical prayers from degenerating into an empty ceremony."[25] We may thus say that the Liturgy is a magnificent, divinely-inspired expression of the Church's *hope*, but that it must at all times be informed and illuminated by the Church's *faith*. Failing this specific information, charity is weakened rather than intensified, even although external dignity may be maintained.

### 4  DEVELOPMENTS IN EUCHARISTIC THEOLOGY

Vonier asserts that the dignity of Catholic worship is safe for all time through the simple fact of the mysteriousness of the Mass. Nonetheless, one's concept of eucharistic theology exercises a profound influence over the whole tenor of one's interior life, and in looking towards the future it is necessary to take into account some of the views which have been expressed concerning the essence of the holy Sacrifice.

Now in speaking of the Berullian reaction to Christian humanism as developed in the seventeenth century, we have already remarked on the French concept of the eucharistic Sacrifice which Père de Condren did so much to propagate.[26] Up to the time of the Reformation, no one had considered it necessary to question the traditional teaching of the Church about the sacrament-sacrifice of the Body and Blood of Christ, and Holy Communion had always been looked upon as the means whereby man—made one with the Redeemer through living faith and the baptismal character—ascends towards God. Many theological points in this connexion were elucidated by St. Thomas Aquinas and later confirmed by the Council of Trent in its twenty-second session, yet it seemed by the end of the nineteenth century as though the French theory might prevail, namely the concept of perpetual oblation in terms of the Heavenly Christ alone. Even St. Alphonsus, who was influenced considerably by de Condren, sometimes refers to our Lord as coming down from heaven at the behest of man, but there is nothing remote about his doctrine as a whole. On the contrary, it is one of intimate, confident love, and in this he principally resembles St. Teresa in her great devotion to the Sacrament of the altar.

The principal theories of oblation, developing the Sulpician doctrine and identified with the historical revival at the end of the nineteenth century, were advanced by M. de la Taille, S.J.,[27] and the Abbé Lepin.[28] Subsequently, Dom Anscar Vonier, O.S.B.,[29] defended the sacramental objectivity of the Thomist-Tridentine standpoint against these French innovations, above all in his masterly article entitled "Eucharistic Theology",[30] and in the following chapter of *Sketches and Studies in Theology* he again insists:—

> The Eucharist is not Christ brought down from heaven; the Eucharist is a sacrament, a thing of material elements which are changed through transubstantiation into an infinitely high thing, the very elements which make Christ in heaven what he is. . . . God has the power to make the same reality exist under two different modes of being, *the natural mode*, as Christ possesses it in heaven, and the sacramental mode of the Catholic Eucharist. There does not seem to be elsewhere another instance of such a transposing of reality; the Eucharist is the only complete and clear case of which we know; in fact the Eucharist is what it is through that very transposition of reality from one order of being to another order of being. The difference between Christ's Eucharistic state of being and his *natural state* of being may be called infinite if we like, since it is the greatest possible difference, but the underlying reality is one and the same.[31]

In a modern synthesis by Antonio Piolanti, Rector of the Pontifical Lateran University, it has been objected that Vonier —in distinguishing the sacramental aspect of the holy Eucharist from what is present by concomitance—neglects "the interior element, in which lies the soul of every sacrifice".[32] To this, however, one may reply in the words of Pius XII that "the unbloody immolation . . . on the altar . . . is performed by the priest alone, and by the priest in so far as he acts in the name of Christ, not in so far as he represents the faithful. Precisely because the priest places the divine victim on the altar, he presents

it as an oblation to God the Father for the glory of the blessed
Trinity and for the benefit of the whole Church";[33] again, that
"the external rite of sacrifice must, of its very nature, be a sign
of internal worship", similarly that "what is signified by the
sacrifice of the New Law is that supreme homage by which
Christ, the principal offerer, and with him and through him all
his mystical members, pay due honour and veneration to God".[34]
Many people feel that these theological differences are of small
practical consequence; yet they do in fact exert the maximum
influence, one way or the other, on the nature of Christian hope
and the mystical concepts stemming therefrom. With these
thoughts in mind, let us now turn to the greatest of all our
modern mystics, St. Thérèse of Lisieux.


5   St. Therese of Lisieux: Flower of Divine Grace

On 25th December 1886 Thérèse Martin received the eucharistic
grace which transposed her interior life from the level of tears
and scruples to one of heroic self-immolation in union with
Jesus Christ. From then on, although barely fourteen years old
at the time, she knew that she might rely on Jesus for everything, and this by reason of her own frailty together with the
infinite compassion of his Sacred Heart. "Our Lord, newly born,"
she says, "turned this darkness of mine into a flood of light;
born to share my human weakness, he brought me the strength
and courage I needed. . . . My tears dried up at their source."[35]
Later, during the first year after her religious profession in
Carmel, the full measure of her confidence was temporarily
clouded by the doubt as to whether her involuntary faults and
failings were an obstacle to divine grace, but on this occasion
our Lord reassured her by means of the Franciscan retreat-master,
Père Alexis Prou, thus launching her "in full sail on the ocean

of confidence and love".[36] Explaining this, she says: "When I'm frightened, I simply curl up; when I'm appealed to by love, I can go ahead at full speed".[37] Later, too, she observes: "Our Lord has ascended into heaven, so I can only follow him by means of the traces he has left behind him. But they are so full of light, so full of fragrance! One glance at the holy Gospel, and the life of Jesus becomes a perfume that fills the very air I breathe. I know at once which way to run."[38]

The prayer of simple regard, as we have seen, had for centuries been the predominant feature in French piety, but all too often as a means of lazy abstraction and even of escape from earthly reality. St. Thérèse, too, practised the prayer of simple regard, but with this difference: the object of her regard was Jesus Christ *according as he had revealed himself upon this earth.* After the time of her entry into Carmel, aridity and fatigue afflicted her so much that no other form of mental prayer could have been sustained in any case; yet her personal attachment to Jesus of the Gospel remained so constant, so intense, that in all things she was directed by his Spirit. Loving a person, as St. Alphonsus Liguori points out, means that we believe "all that proceeds from the lips of that person. Consequently, the more a soul loves Jesus Christ, the more lively and unshaken is her faith."[39] St. Thérèse, then, looked first to the Child Jesus, secondly to his Holy Face in the mystery of the Passion, and even when her soul was entering upon eternity her one thought was to spend her heaven doing good upon earth. The rest could wait until the mission of Jesus the Redeemer was complete. In her own case, moreover, this special Christo-centric urge dated from an evening by the seaside when she was little more than seven years old. She and Pauline had made their way on to a rock, so as to watch the setting sun and its long track of light over the water. "For a long time I sat there thinking about this track of light and of its heavenly counterpart," she says, "the grace which pierces the darkness and guides the little white-sailed ship on its course. Sitting there beside Pauline, I made a resolve that I would always think of our Lord as watching me, and travel straight on in his line of vision till I came safe to the shore of my heavenly country."[40]

Sometimes it is asserted that St. Thérèse was not a contemplative at all, still less a mystic of the quality of St. Teresa and St. John of the Cross, since everything about her remained so natural, so child-like, so perfectly ordinary. Since her ambition, while on earth, was to remain as the "insignificant grain of sand, trodden down by all who passed by", what then was the secret of her confidence, of her absolute conviction, that she could after all "be lifted up to heaven in the arms of Jesus",[41] in which event there would be no need for her to grow bigger but, rather, smaller? Child of love that she was, she invariably secured her own way—even down to the grace of Holy Communion five times a week, some twenty years before the revised eucharistic legislation of St. Pius X—the secret being that Jesus himself inspired her wishes, then rejoiced with her in their fulfilment. The fact that she was habitually docile to the initiative of the Holy Spirit—consequently that the path she trod was the essential mystical way of pure faith and hope, called by St. John of the Cross "the obscure night"—has been revealed in the words which she wrote about her retreat made before profession, a retreat made in great aridity of spirit. "I always have the feeling," she says, "that our Lord doesn't supply me with provisions for my journey—he just gives me food unexpectedly when and as I need it; I find it there without knowing how it got there. It simply comes to this, that our Lord dwells unseen in the depths of my miserable soul, and so works upon me by grace that I can always find out what he wants me to do at this particular moment."[42] Later, she defined prayer as "a vast supernatural force, which opens out my heart and binds me close to Jesus";[43] but we must not think of this in terms of sensible consolation, as described for example in the fourth mansion of St. Teresa. Almost all her time in choir was spent in turning fatigue and involuntary distractions to supernatural account, using even her spells of drowsiness as the means of intensifying her child-like confidence in Jesus alone. "I go to sleep without meaning to," she explains, "I'm like a bird that shuts its eyes and puts its head under its wing when darkness comes on. . . . When I recollect myself, I don't get distressed over it; with my heart still at rest, I take up again my task of love."[44]

Now love is a quality which must always develop or intensify in this life, in order that it may attain its maximum supernatural effectiveness, and the manner in which this takes place conforms itself intimately with our individual psychology. Through sanctifying grace, we participate in the divinity of Christ, we *are* Christ, but without the least diminution in our own self-being. So long as we live, therefore, the theological virtues must continue their work of perfecting the powers inherent to this self-being, purifying and elevating them in readiness for the experience of eternity. This, however, is no mere abstraction: it is, above all, an individual love-story between Jesus Christ and every soul for whom he has died, written moreover in as many different idioms. As we are, so will the manhood of Jesus attract us; and in the case of St. Thérèse one is struck particularly by the progressive maturity of her affective powers, according as these were acted upon by the mystery of Calvary. Thus soon after the decisive grace of Christmas, 1886, a further interior illumination was granted to the young Thérèse as she looked at a picture of Jesus Crucified and observed the unheeded flow of the blood from one of his hands. From now on, she would "stand, in spirit, at the foot of the Cross and gather up this saving balm that distilled from it, always with the intention of applying it to the need of souls".[45] Pranzini's repentance renewed this

determination, increased this longing for souls. What had begun
as an experiment, now became a life-work. Thus affective love
and effective love, like wisdom and grace, went from strength
to strength in Thérèse's resolute little heart, until gradually the
whole world came to be included in the scope of her mission,
including the souls of priests as the special objects of her self-
immolating attentions. By 1890, she knew that souls can be
saved not only by means of voluntary mortification but even
more effectively through passive sufferings. In pure faith and
hope, quite simply, the little flower *must look at Jesus* whilst
undergoing these purifications, such moments of oneness with
him being the source of all supernatural fruitfulness.[46] Most
important of all, however, was her realization that the fraternal
charity demanded by life in community is wholly beyond our
natural resources, therefore that Jesus himself must take command
of the situation. "I am not just to love my neighbours as myself,"
she says, "I am to love them as Jesus loves them, and will love
them till the end of time. Dear Lord," she then exclaims," . . .
that must mean that you yourself go on loving them in and
through me—you know it wouldn't be possible in any other
way."[47] Truly the perfecting of God's image in the soul of
Thérèse Martin was a masterpiece of delicacy on the part of his
merciful Love! Compared with this, her outward act of self-
oblation to the blessed Trinity was of no more than secondary
importance, marking as it did the special call to spiritual marriage
and subsequent night of the spirit, which in her case ceased only
in the hour of her death.

Those who discern the resemblance between the "Little Way"
of St. Thérèse and the "Ascent of Mount Carmel" as described
by St. John of the Cross, tend to assume that the first is derived
from the second, especially as St. Thérèse was so attracted by
the writings of the Mystical Doctor. On the other hand, when
trying to associate her with the four waters or the seven mansions

of St. Teresa, the task to them seems an impossible one. Almost certainly, however, the "Little Way" and its subsidiary teaching owes its doctrine directly to the Holy Spirit, the many resemblances being no more than of supernatural coincidence. As for her personal interior journey, there is every indication that she and Céline enjoyed the infused consolations of St. Teresa's fourth mansion as early as the year 1887, that the night of sense became complete for her as from the time of entering Carmel, and that she had experienced the first delicate touches of substantial union by the time of her religious profession. The grace associated with the retreat given by Père Alexis Prou must certainly have had its mystical counterpart, bringing her to the degree of substantial union wherein "the soul is asleep, fast asleep, as regards the world and itself".[48] Perfection, as we have seen in the course of this study, always consists first in bringing the will into perfect conformity with the divine will (through charity and the moral virtues), secondly in the transformation of our understanding and memory (through pure faith and hope). St. Teresa of Avila lived for ten years after attaining to the perfection of substantial union and spiritual marriage with Jesus Christ, St. John of the Cross thirteen years. St. Thérèse, on the other hand, by remaining in the night of the spirit until the end, is a special consolation to the vast multitude of God's children who daily pass from the limits of time and space to the new experience of eternity in Christ Jesus, and that was always her own ambition. "Ought not Christ to have suffered these things, and so to enter into his glory" (Luke xxiv 26)? That was what our Lord asked the disciples on the road to Emmaus, and in that simple question is the essence of all mystical experience contained.

[1]Vonier, *Collected Works*, Vol. 2, p. 53.
[2]Op. cit., p. 52.
[3]Vonier, *Sketches and Studies in Theology*, p. 58.
[4]*Rerum novarum*, 1891, and *Quadragesimo anno*, 1931.

12

[5] *The Way of St. Alphonsus Liguori*, edited by B. Ulanov, p. 132.

[6] Op. cit., p. 143.

[7] Op. cit., p. 346.

[8] Op. cit., p. 269: "On Prayer".

[9] Op. cit., p. 85.

[10] Cf. *Homo Apostolicus*, Appendix I.

[11] Cf. Op. cit., Appendix I, 10.

[12] Cf. *Praxis*, n. 221, also *True Spouse*, xv, 2.

[13] *The Way of St. Alphonsus Liguori*, p. 351.

[14] Scheeben, *Mysteries of Christianity*, p. 419.

[15] *In The Whole Christ*, pp. 163 and 164.

[16] Cf. Lercaro, *Methods of Mental Prayer*, p. 253.

[17] *The Way of St. Alphonsus Liguori*, p. 351.

[18] *In The Whole Christ*, p. 164.

[19] Spiritual Maxim, No. 218; p. 370, L. G. & Co.

[20] Cf. Pourrat, Vol. 4, pp. 509–14.

[21] The English translation by Michael Turner is called *I Believe*, published by Geoffrey Chapman, London, 1959.

[22] *Sketches and Studies in Theology*, p. 151.

[23] C.T.S., London, 1943; para. 88.

[24] C.T.S., London, 1947; para. 186.

[25] C.T.S., London, 1947; para. 187.

[26] Author of *L'Idée du Sacerdoce et du sacrifice de Jésus-Christ*.

[27] Author of *Mysterium Fidei*.

[28] Author of *L'Idée du Sacrifice de la Messe*.

[29] Author of *Key to Doctrine of the Eucharist*.

[30] First published in *The Tablet*, then in *Sketches and Studies*.

[31] *Sketches and Studies in Theology*, pp. 96–7.

[32] *The Holy Eucharist*, p. 104.

[33] *Mediator Dei*, C.T.S., London, para. 96.

[34] Op. cit., para. 98.

[35] *Autobiography of a Saint*, Ch. XV, pp. 126–7.

[36] Op. cit., Ch. XXVIII, p. 211.

[37] Loc. cit.

[38] Op. cit., Ch. XI, p. 311.

[39] *The Way of St. Alphonsus Liguori*, pp. 177–8.

[40] *Autobiography of a Saint*, Ch. VII, pp. 74–5.

[41] Op. cit., Ch. XXI, p. 248.

[42] Op. cit., Ch. XXVI, pp. 198–9.

[43] Op. cit., Ch. XXXVII, p. 289.

[44] Op. cit., Ch. XXX, p. 240.

[45] Op. cit., Ch. XV, p. 128.

[46] Cf. Letter 107.

[47] *Autobiography of a Saint*, Ch. XXXIV, p. 266.

[48] *Interior Castle*, Mansion 5; p. 121, Baker.

# EPILOGUE

## Towards The New Charity

THESE PAGES have been completed at the time when the Church, obedient to the command of His Holiness, Pope Paul VI, has reassembled for the second Session of the Vatican Council; and it is with particular gratitude, therefore, that we should look back over the centuries of the Christian era and marvel anew at the unfailing victory of divine grace over evil, still more at the unfailing compassion of our Redeemer in relation to human frailty. Mankind changes but little, for all that the outward achievement of individuals or of nations may astonish our senses and compel our admiration. Sooner or later each must die, each must account for the stewardship of the graces offered to him while still on earth, and in that decisive hour there is no opportunity for self-deception. As St. Paul says, "it is appointed unto men once to die, and, after this, the judgement" (Heb. ix. 27).

Everything of eternal value thus depends on man's readiness to accept the gift of grace and to recognize the Son of God and his blessed Mother, through whom this gift has been bestowed. Therefore the story of the last two thousand years—when examined objectively—must surely convince every Christian of good will of the vital rôle that the Church must play, both in protecting the timeless Christological doctrines against error and in presenting these doctrines to God's children in a form best suited to their individual needs, the scope of their intelligence, and the generosity of their hearts. No revival of charity, no abiding mystical glory moreover, has ever been achieved without deep personal devotion to the Humanity of our Lord—

the Humanity deified by reason of its hypostatic assumption by the Eternal Word—and that is why man if truly self-loving must first *find himself* in Christ Jesus.

Since the time of the Protestant Reformation, in particular, we have seen how the spirit of falsehood has tried to impede this joyful realization of self in Christ, but again how truth has gradually re-asserted itself in the minds of men following years of conflicting opinions and even of bitter controversy. We have seen how the deeper realities of mystical theology have been obscured in a threefold way: by inadequate philosophical concepts; by the attempt to divorce them from Jesus Christ and the mysteries of his life on earth; finally by the tendency to despise the divine flesh and blood of our Redeemer prior to the Resurrection and Ascension, and to make the blessed Eucharist into a "heavenly sacrifice" instead of a sacrament-sacrifice adapted to the needs of man in his earthly condition. Today, however, we can rejoice no less at the fearless way in which the popes of the twentieth century have sought to re-direct the attention of philosophers and theologians to the constant teaching of the Church, ensuring too that the timeless precision of the Latin language be universally preserved. Most significant of all, perhaps, are the words of Pope Pius XII concerning false spirituality: "It is . . . blasphemous," he said, "to assert that the contemplation of the physical Heart of Christ is an obstacle to our reaching the innermost love of God, and that the soul is delayed thereby on the road that leads to the height of the virtues. This false mysticism the Church utterly rejects";[1] and again: ". . . The whole validity of the physical Heart of Jesus as a natural symbol of the Person of the Word, *rests upon the fundamental truth* of the hypostatic union. He, who denies this truth, resurrects those false beliefs which the Church has rejected on more than one occasion, because they contradict the doctrine that there is one Person in Christ, while the two natures remain distinct and entire."[2] The martyrdom of St. Maximus the Confessor may here be recalled.

Amongst the lesser-known Carmelite nuns of the past two centuries who have contributed most to the true principle of Christo-centric mysticism, special mention must be made of St. Teresa Margaret of the Sacred Heart of Jesus, who died in 1770 at the age of twenty-three in the Florence Carmel, also of Sister Elizabeth of the Trinity who died in 1906 at the age of twenty-six in the Carmel of Dijon, and whose cause for beatification is under consideration. St. Teresa Margaret followed the path of ecstatic love and of perfect self-devotion to her sisters in religion; Sister Elizabeth of the Trinity, while basing her conscious thinking on the Pauline doctrine of configuration to Christ Crucified, was carried swiftly into the way of pure faith and hope, and attained on her death-bed to the degree of assured oneness with Christ and his mystical body which usually precedes the grace of transforming union in him. We must thank God also for the countless angels of peace in modern times who exemplify the teaching of Pius XII that "the most active forms of busy work can be united with the rare riches of the interior life".[3]

Amongst the great dogmatic writers of the age, who have contributed most to the cause of mystical theology, special mention has been made in this book of Matthias Scheeben[4] and Abbot Vonier, O.S.B.;[5] and in this same category may be placed Émile Mersch, S.J.,[6] also Jean Mouroux, whose emphasis on the personal aspect of the teaching of St. John of the Cross is quite outstanding. The powers of darkness do not cease to attack our spirit of faith, but cannot touch us whilst we shelter in the Sacred Heart; theological hope is still in travail, more deeply than ever before, but knows with St. Paul that its trust will never be confounded. In conclusion, then, let us recall the magnificent words of St. Leo the Great as quoted by the late Holy Father in *Aeterna Dei Sapientia:*—

The faithful, wholly and singly, are God's temple; and just as his temple is perfect in the whole, so must it be perfect in the individual. For although all the members are not equally beautiful, nor can there be parity of merits in so great a variety of parts, nevertheless the bond of charity makes them all alike sharers in the beauty of the whole. For they are all united in the fellowship of holy love, and though they do not all make use of the same gifts of grace, they nevertheless rejoice with one another in the good things which are theirs. Nor can the object of their love be anything which bears no relation to themselves, for in the very fact of rejoicing in another's progress, they are enriched in their own growth.[7]

Nowhere is this more true than in the universal field of Christian mystical experience, Amen.

[1] *Haurietis Aquas*, C.T.S., London, 1956, para. 57.
[2] Op. cit., para 59.
[3] See Courtois, *The States of Perfection*, trans. J. O'Flynn, (Gills, Dublin), p. 181.
[4] Author of *Nature and Grace*, *Mysteries of Christianity*, etc.
[5] Author of some 15 theological works, articles, sketches, etc.
[6] Author of *The Theology of the Mystical Body*, etc.
[7] *Aeterna Dei Sapientia*, C.T.S., London, 1961, para. 31.